Japan: film image

Richard N Tucker

JAPAN: FILM IMAGE

Studio Vista London

To Jane

The author would like to thank all those who have helped in so many ways in the preparation of this book. Grateful thanks are given for advice, information, research, typing and manuscript checking and, most of all, for tolerance, understanding and encouragement, to the following people: Toyoji Kuroda (Secretary-General, UniJapan Film), T. Moriwaki (Japan Audio-visual Educational Association), Miss K. Rowland and the staff of the Information Department of the Japanese Embassy in London, John Gillett and all his colleagues at the British Film Institute, my colleagues at the Scottish Film Council, and Jane Williamson, Erica Hunningher, Elizabeth Macdonald, Muriel Falla and Peggy Murdoch.

As regards the poems, 'Modern Senryu', 'Silent, But' by Tsuboi Shigeji, 'Farewell Before Dawn' by Nakano Shigeharu, 'Stars' and 'Tourist Japan' by Takenaka Iku, all translated by Geoffrey Bownas and Anthony Thwaite, are reprinted from *The Penguin Book of Japanese Verse*, © Geoffrey Bownas and Anthony Thwaite 1964, by kind permission of Penguin Books Ltd. All other poems have been translated by the author.

Front cover: Toshiro Mifune as Tsubaki Sanjuro in Akira Kurosawa's
Sanjuro (Toho, 1962)
Back cover: Yukio Mishima's *Rites of love and death* (1965)

First published in London 1973 by
Studio Vista, 35 Red Lion Square, London WC1R 4SG
Set in Ehrhardt 11 pt
Filmset and printed by
BAS Printers Limited, Wallop, Hampshire

Contents

Preface

In approaching the task of writing about the Japanese cinema one becomes increasingly aware of the enormous scale of that nation's film industry. Looking at Japanese film outside Japan is like looking at the crystalline glory of an iceberg without knowledge of the vast volume that lies hidden. Since the success of *Rashomon* the attention of audiences and critics has turned slowly towards the products of this, the world's largest cinema industry. The sad fact is that we have such a small sample by which to judge the overall quality of the films and often too little knowledge of the cultural background from which these films have sprung.

To a large extent this book arises from a personal response to Japanese films. Apart from the few examples which had achieved distribution in Europe by 1960 my first real exposure to Japanese cinema came during a number of visits to that country between 1959 and 1963. Even a brief sampling of the Japanese domestic fare is enough to indicate that those films which are exported, albeit the best of their kind, are not necessarily representative of the majority of the cinematic output. Seen in a Japanese context it is also obvious that there are elements within the films which are meaningful only to those with a Japanese cultural background. It would be impossible for any book to give to the reader an instant understanding of all the cultural modifiers implicit in Japanese film. What this book attempts to do is to set out a few pointers which might serve as an introductory guide and hopefully increase the understanding and enjoyment of Japanese films.

Any writing on the Japanese cinema is likely to be influenced by the work of Donald Richie, who for many years has so tirelessly championed the work of the industry as a whole and that of Kurosawa in particular. Though I take issue with some of his attitudes and judgements I must acknowledge a great debt of gratitude to him for his exhaustive historical work – if any of his ideas have become absorbed in my own by a process of intellectual osmosis then I willingly offer him the credit for these.

The first section is a brief survey of the development of the Japanese cinema intended to provide a context by which to judge later works. My intention is not to construct a complete history – for this the reader should turn to Donald Richie – but simply to mark the key points along the line of development. It would be the job of another book to examine the early work of great masters such as Ozu and Mizoguchi, and to re-assess the value of that brilliant director of sword-play dramas, Daisuke Ito.

The central section selects a limited number of directors as exemplars of my thesis that an ethical spectrum can be observed throughout Japanese cinema. The apparent omission of directors such as Gosho, Naruse and Imai arises from the small number of their films that have been seen outside Japan, rather than any reflection of their value as creative artists. The same criteria used to outline the concept of the ethical spectrum can be applied with equal ease to their work.

The final section contains a brief over-view of the current trends in Japanese cinema, with its insistence on sex and violence, and attempts to provide some pointers to cultural and social influences which might have given rise to this emphasis within the films.

In such a small space as a book allows, one can only skip through the large number of films produced using a few examples as stepping-stones. Having written this book with both an abiding passion for Japanese cinema and an awareness of its weaknesses I can only hope that it will stimulate more people to look at more Japanese films with enjoyment and understanding.

October 1972
Richard N. Tucker

Part one
A brief history

1 Silent films with voices

Castle-on-the-heights

Summer grasses;
Of strong soldiers dreams
The aftermath.

Matsuo Basho 1644–1694

In 1542 the wreck of a Portuguese ship brought the Occidental world suddenly into the life of the Japanese. The same year Francis Xavier, the Jesuit
missionary, arrived in Japan and began the spread of Christianity. Over the
following years the Dutch and the Spanish followed the Portuguese. Long
experienced in colonial policy, these countries began to make serious inroads
into Japan with the establishment of trading empires. Japan felt threatened,
not only by these powers but also by Russia, now advanced to her eastern
seaboard, and by Britain gaining influence in India.

The Shogun, a sort of generalissimo who really ruled Japan in the name of
the Emperor, countered the foreign threat by closing down the country
completely, by issuing in 1624 the 'Edict of Isolation'. For nearly two hundred
and thirty years Japan was hermetically sealed from the rest of the world.*

It was during these two centuries that some of the greatest advances in
man's scientific and industrial knowledge took place. When the seal on the
country was eventually broken in 1853 by the arrival of the American ex-
pedition under Commodore Matthew Perry, Japan was seen to have advanced
a little but had a very long way to catch up. Once the barriers were down the
West could look into this strange country, but conversely Japan could look
out to a world that was rapidly industrializing. To survive in this suddenly
enlarged context Japan had to compete and to compete she had to beat the
rest of the world at its own game. The Japanese have throughout their
history learned from others. One aspect remains consistent through this
learning process; each time Japan learns something it is only a short period of
time before she becomes the master rather than the pupil.

When Matthew Perry eventually arrived in what is now Tokyo, after
being tricked many times by the Japanese petty officials, he presented a
collection of gifts to the Emperor. Amongst the many objects he chose to
represent the best of America was one which was to be the direct root of the
cinema in Japan: a Daguerreotype outfit. That photography was to start as a
gift to the Emperor may have had a great deal to do with the nature of the
early development of the cinema.

*For a simple account of this period see *Japan: the story of a nation* by Edwin O. Reischauer.

The arrival of 'the foreign devils' in Japan was not a smooth process, but a story full of arrogance and blood. Eventually the Shogun was deposed and the Emperor restored to real power.

1868 saw the beginning of the Meiji period. At sixteen years of age Emperor Meiji gave up the title 'Mikado' and moved the court from Kyoto to Yedo, which was then renamed Tokyo. The changes that were made in the following years must be among the most cataclysmic that have ever happened to any nation, for in less than thirty years Japan was to make a leap forward equivalent to a couple of centuries of Western development. As well as adopting and adapting many of the Western ways a great deal of the 'old' Japan was retained, the resulting confusion of impression being still strongly visible today.

Imagine then this strange world of contrasting styles. Such was the strength of interest in the West that much was adopted piecemeal without any sense of stylistic incongruity. Bowler hats and straw boaters were worn with the formal *kimono*, large pocket watches became a problem in a costume which did not have a waistcoat pocket, and spectacles achieved such status as signs of learning that they were worn irrespective of the wearer's eyesight. With a population eager for knowledge of anything to do with the West the introduction of the magic lantern was a godsend. Here there were no language problems and the common man could see with his own eyes what things were like in that strange land across the sea. Most of the lantern material came from France, and the French entrepreneurs were not slow to make profit out of this interest. By 1894 there was a regular circuit of touring magic-lantern shows.

Edison's Kinetoscope was first demonstrated to a wondering Japanese public in 1896 and in the same year his Vitascope and Lumière's *cinematographes* were imported and studied, though it wasn't until the following year that the general public saw the cinematograph. When cinema arrived a very particular set of circumstances arose that were to condition its development. It was already in a fairly sophisticated stage of development before the Japanese saw it and they had let others make all the initial mistakes, but more important in social terms, it was introduced at an official level. The first film was shot in Japan in 1897 but it was not shown until 1899 so that two years after the public had been seeing films, they were now to see their own product. The screening was held in the Kabuki-za, the Kabuki theatre in Tokyo, and this set the seal on the cinema. The performance was graced by Royalty and the setting of the Kabuki theatre as the home of the motion picture meant that it was the medium for the upper middle class and the rich. This is in strong contrast with the beginnings of cinema in the West, especially in the States where the cinema was entertainment for the common man, an adjunct of the music-halls. Japan never experienced the equivalent of the Nickelodeon.

Initially the growth of indigenous cinema was hindered because of the need to send all the film back to France for processing. With typical tenacity the Japanese soon set about building their own industry. The first motion picture camera was industrially produced in 1900, just over three years after they had first seen moving pictures, and by this time their first processing laboratory had been opened.

As in the West the overpowering interest was initially in newsreel material. The medium had not yet been sufficiently developed as a dramatic vehicle, and the Japanese were willing to watch any film from any other country. In the same year as the making of their first camera, they equipped a newsreel-cameraman and packed him off to China to film the Boxer Revolution (1900).

Being housed originally in the Kabuki theatre and with the availability of actors and ready-made scripts, it was only natural that the first dramatic films produced in Japan should be versions of famous and popular Kabuki plays. This placed two conditions on the making of films. Having grown out of a theatrical background the film accepted one of the precepts of the theatre – all the players must be male. Such playing is far from being a display of transvestite behaviour, but rather a subtle and refined portrayal of the essence of the female characteristics in the Kabuki plays. Thus the cinema accepted without question that all parts should be played by men, and it was twenty years before women appeared in films. The second condition imposed by the theatrical background was the use of the *benshi*.

The *benshi* is the narrator or commentator who has a central function in the Kabuki theatre and the Bunraku puppet theatre. Sitting at one side of the stage the *benshi* tells the audience what is happening, he fills in all the details that cannot be seen on the stage, he reports action and can even inform the audience what the characters are thinking – a sort of public interior monologue. As an actor in any well-known play, he would be appreciated more for the style of the delivery than for the intellectual content of his narrative, which is delivered in a stylized fashion, the words long and drawn out in a chant, the total effect being like the pulse of the play. He could control its pace and emotional temper. It was therefore natural that the *benshi* should be employed to narrate and comment on the films of the Kabuki plays.

Industrially this was viable since it saved the expense of having to print subtitles. It also simplified much for the directors and actors; if they failed to get something across to the audience visually the *benshi* could always tell them. At first this meant that the industry boomed because it could put across, to a wide public, exciting plays in a form that they knew and accepted. Eventually it was to be an enormous handicap to the film-makers.

Since much of the film that was being shown came from other countries the *benshi* served another important function. As a commentator he was able to explain to the audience all those little things that they would have missed because of the cultural differences between the countries. One oft-quoted example is the newsreel of the Czar of Russia arriving in Paris: the Crown Prince of Japan in a private view of the newsreel confused the Czar with the coachman who was in the superior position on the top of the coach.

It was very easy for the *benshi* to dominate the presentation of the show. The Japanese liked to be instructed and these men lost few opportunities for comment. Having declared all the relevant detail in a scene, this indefatigable narrator would go on to describe all the irrelevant trivia which the audience could very well see for themselves: 'the sun is shining, the trees are bending in the wind . . .' etc. As the film industry established itself firmly in the life of the people so the *benshi* established what seemed to be a permanent position. Because films might arrive without a synopsis, or through the personal taste of the particular *benshi*, there was no real control on the information that was fed to the audience. It was possible to see the same film material several times and to get different interpretations. At the height of their popularity the *benshi* for a theatre would often be advertised in bigger letters than the film being shown.

Unfortunately as the film grew towards maturity, developing a language and a grammar of its own, the strength and support of the *benshi* became a strangle-hold. There had been no need for the Japanese film-maker to do anything more than load the camera and run a full magazine of stock from a single camera position while the actors emoted in front of the lens. Griffith and others had discovered how to correlate emotional states visually, and were using these devices to call forth emotional responses from their audiences.* Not so the Japanese. Who needed such devices when all the work was done for them? It is noticeable however that the Japanese cinema is still sparing in its use of the close-up, and will use significant action rather than dialogue to convey information.

The *benshis'* hold on the industry was so strong that they not only repressed the development of film techniques, but once sound came along in 1927 they decided to fight it, and such was their tenacity that they stayed in the cinemas until 1932. Some silent films were still being made, but the cold wind of unemployment was blowing round these seated figures. They could not talk over the new talking-pictures, however much they tried, so they called a strike of all the *benshi*. This was a fatal move for them, since nobody asked them to come back and it gave a new freedom for the Japanese film.

From these beginnings grew the Japanese cinema. From the earliest newsreels they progressed to sections of Kabuki plays (first filmed by a department store photographic section). It was Shozo Makino who first recognized the business potential of the cinema. He was a small-time theatre owner who occasionally made some one-reel Kabuki stories until he discovered a then unknown actor in a poor-grade Kabuki troop. This may have been the first case outside the USA of the 'creation' of a star, for Makino nurtured Matsunosuke Onoe into a dominant position within the Japanese film. Makino and his 'star' approached Kenichi Kawaura, an entrepreneur whose company had first brought the cinematograph to Japan, and the mixture gelled into a fantastic box-office success. In 1908 Kawaura built the first film studio in Japan, after having studied the way things were being done in the USA. Suddenly, with the impetus of star appeal, film production became a commercial possibility. The public following of their new-found hero was enormous and this placed great pressure on the studios. In the first two years Matsunosuke Onoe, under the direction of Makino, made 170 films. This meant that at times he must have been producing a reel a day. It is easy to look at the films now and see that they were done by having a *benshi* on the set telling a story to which the actors simply improvised, there being no changes of camera position, but as will be seen later this type of productivity may be inherent in the character of the Japanese film-maker, for a modern company with all the mechanical trappings of the modern film can still turn out two full-length feature films a week from its studios in Tokyo.

The American film-makers were already well advanced in the art of telling stories with the camera. Edwin S. Porter had already made his *Great train robbery* and *A Day in the life of an American cowboy*. Although this must have been realized by the Japanese directors, they adopted strange methods to correct the old-fashioned look. Makino took to running his camera at half speed, with the result that his characters shot around the screen like demented beings – he could even get more story into a single reel that way. Others, in trying to be modern simply turned to the *Shimpa*, another theatrical form, a sort of debased, yet still stylized, version of the kabuki. A more modern 'social realism' theatre, the *Shingeki*, had just begun to emerge in Japan and the early cinema borrowed heavily from this. The first contributions that the *Shingeki* made to the cinema were versions of Tolstoy's stories, since Japan at this time had not yet developed a native literary talent in this new style, so a great number of foreign works were adapted for the stage and film.

Shingeki used all the trappings of the Western theatre, including the

*Kurt Pintus in *Das Kinobuch* (Verlag der Arche, Zurich) reports coming across a narrator in a cinema in Desau, Saxony, as late as 1917. He stood in front of the screen describing the images.

proscenium arch, and this suited the direct transposition of the plays on to film. The camera was maintained solidly in a 'stage front' position and the action was observed as though through the proscenium arch, partly because the Japanese equated the cinema with the theatre and saw no justification for a change of camera position – other than being able to afford a seat at the front of the stalls. When a closer shot registers in the mind of the audience as a cash relation then there is little chance of the director revealing the mental states of his characters with the camera.

At first, directors resisted developments, despite knowledge of what was happening overseas, but the change had to come eventually and it came from those who had studied in America and Russia, especially Henry Kotani and Thomas Kurihara. At first these modern men with all the modern techniques made movies that were not liked by much of the public – not because they were too modern but because they were not serious enough. The Japanese tend to take some aspects of life very seriously. At that time it seems that since they had paid for something they still related to the theatre, and they all knew that theatre was very serious, they demanded that the film promoted in them deep emotions and great thought.

Kotani and Kurihara managed to introduce to the Japanese audiences all the techniques of the American cinema but only after learning their lessons did they give their audiences just what they wanted. Kurihara made a very sad film *The Lasciviousness of the viper* and Kotani made a great success out of making modern films using Kabuki actors – the best of both worlds, blending modern stories and American techniques with the popularity of the recognized film stars.

Thus very slowly a change began in the hidebound cinema. Those elements which had been the strength of the cinema in its early days had quickly ossified and were now threatening the future of the movie as a living art. The new directors were just beginning to be able to move the camera, but it was still basically locked into the middle of the theatre stalls. Women had not yet appeared in front of the cameras and the whole process was enclosed in the glass-walled studios.

1921 was to be the watershed for the Japanese cinema.

2 Exit benshi, enter beauty

The Firefly Hunt

The lost child crying
And crying grasping
At the fireflies.

Ryushi 1691–1758

1921 was the year of two great liberations for the Japanese cinema. In the first instance it was freed from having to use *onnagatu*, the male actors who played women's parts. Women had appeared on the screen, real flesh and blood women, women in whom the public could believe. The small group of film-makers who had been trained overseas, who knew that film could approach reality, demanded the appearance of women. The result was astonishing. Suddenly the public, which by now was largely middle class, had characters with whom they could identify. Onoe, who had held the centre of the public's interest, now began to slide from popularity. New stars were in the ascendency.

One of the difficulties was that initially they all became stars, for such was the interest that every new woman was heralded as a public wonder, four thousand copies of a photograph of Sumiko Kurishima being sold in one day in Tokyo. Under this type of competition the old-guard of the Kabuki actors knew that their days were numbered.

Secondly, the directors of the time used this phenomenon as an opportunity to make radical changes in the styles of screen acting. Although some of these early films look somewhat exaggerated in acting style to the modern eye it must be remembered that until two or three years previously all screen acting had been based on the stylization of the Kabuki. The audiences had not demanded anything different, nor did they expect the pictures to look 'real'. They were aware that the camera will only show the surface of things and were happy with the outsize world and the outsize characters depicted in the films. The next move made by the film-makers was to take the cameras out of the studios and theatres and make films on location.

Minoru Murata has the distinction of being the man who made the first really important Japanese film. In 1921 *Souls on the road* was released. Murata had made the film almost entirely on location, he had used women and, perhaps most important of all, he had blended these elements with a camera and acting style that was naturalistic, restrained and evocative of mood, displaying a maturity not seen before in Japanese films. Others had used location before, others had seen and studied American cinema, but it was Murata who first managed to master all these elements.

It is difficult, perhaps, to understand just how great a change this represents in the development of a nation's cinema. It must be remembered that by 1921 Japan was at least fifteen years behind the major film industries. She had no Griffith, no Gance, no man of genius who could lift the film out of those traditions that were slowly strangling it. It is therefore even more amazing when one considers the form and the content of *Souls on the road*. The film is made up of two stories which are woven together without any literary links and only bonded by mood. One of the stories is of two convicts seeking refuge, the other of a man's return home penniless but with a wife and daughter. The first was one of the many adaptations of Gorky's *Lower depths* that have been done both in the theatre and the cinema. Murata structures his film as a set of undetermined events within a given context. A road of one kind or another fills each episode as they flow one into the other, none finishing with a full-stop, none having had a determinable starting point.

The narrative freedom of *Souls on the road* is startling. Shortly after the film has started there is a complex pattern of imaginings and flash-back, even to the extent of a flash-back within a flash-back. Also, at this early stage in film-making Murata was able to use non-literal imagery and symbolism, by leaning heavily on that of Japanese art and poetry.

The impression that this film made on the industry was great. For the first time a film had been made about the poor people of the country. Here was a

Souls on the road (Murata, Shochiku 1921)
Japan's first major film, combining exteriors with a complex narrative style.

realism that could not be achieved in the previous styles of cinema, which were tied to higher social strata. From this point on in the Japanese cinema there was always to be a strong concern for the surface reality of man's existence. The better directors were able to break through that surface, but even if the content might be shallow, the films looked real – mainly because of the reality of the location shooting as opposed to studio sets. Since this time the majority of Japanese films have been made on location with a careful integration of studio shots. Such a custom has given to the films a texture of credible reality.

The flood-gates had been opened and directors began to make films about ordinary people with the common man as a focus. Following the superb model of *Souls on the road* there were many films about 'life as it is', but they tended to concentrate on the tragic and the downtrodden – perhaps because in some way these things are more 'real'. A dark but financially successful air settled over the films of this time.

One recognizes that it is neither a necessary nor a sufficient condition for a film to display a social conscience, but it was inevitable that once the film directors had learned to convey the realities of life, including its sorrows and poverty, it would not be long before someone would use this reality to comment on it.

A new genre emerged around the mid-twenties, whose setting was the middle class. Initially these were light delicate comedies firmly set in ordinary family life. *Shomin-geki*, as this genre was known, was to become the most fruitful area for the whole of Japanese cinema, and was to be taken to its highest form by such directors as Gosho, Naruse, Toyoda, Mizoguchi and

The Izu dancers (Gosho, Shochiku 1933)
Gosho's classic tale of love.

the greatest of them all, Ozu. It was during these formative years of the *Shomin-geki* that Mizoguchi, along with other major powers such as Kinugasa, moved the art of the film towards a state of maturity.

Japan appeared to be entering a new age. Society was affected by the flapper crazes of the twenties as much as Western Europe, and the audiences flocked to the cinemas to see stories of people not unlike themselves. In order to comment on society without arousing the wrath of an increasingly power-ful officialdom the Japanese film discovered that it could use history as a valid analogy to the present. So, once more, a change occurred, this time in 1928. Having discarded historical melodrama for contemporary social realism the directors now found that they could film the Tokogawa period (17th century to 1868) as though it were contemporary society. Such films as Inagaki's *The Wandering gambler* (1928) and *A Swordsman's picture book* (1929) stripped the myth away from history and showed the man in the street to have as much right to live in the world as the government minister or the industrial magnate.

A Page out of order/A Crazy page (1926) and *Crossways* (1928), both by Teinosuke Kinugasa, brought the Japanese film into unexplored realms. The first was expressionistic in technique, and though it followed them by ten years ranks alongside the German expressionist masterpieces. It has been suggested that the style of this film arose fortuitously since in order to get more light into his under-equipped studio Kinugasa painted all the walls silver, thus giving his images a brilliant luminous quality. But that this was not fortuitous was shown by the second of these films. In the first he had introduced subjective camera to his viewers. Now in *Crossways* he demon-

Crossways (Kinugasa, Shochiku and Kinugasa Productions 1928)
Extraordinary scenery and a controlled yet mannered acting style in a genuinely expressionist film.

strated not only that the past can be shown as real but that there is no distinction between past and present, fantasy and reality. Chronological narrative had no part to play in this strange structuring of the film where long scenes of apparently little relation to the plot demanded a far greater degree of participation from the viewer than had been previously expected. Further, not only is the story told in a complex and puzzling fashion but the hero behaves in a way not expected of a strong samurai. Having killed a man he runs to his sister for help, an unheard of response to someone else's death, then later, when the hero discovers that the supposed victim is not dead, he dies from shock.

Despite the outrage felt by the producers the film was a financial success. The audiences regarded the film as a puzzle and it became chic to offer an explanation.

The late twenties correspond closely to the situation in the USA. After twenty years the silent film had developed a language with grammar and syntax all of which was soon to be threatened by the introduction of sound. In 1927 the feature film *Reimei* had been released with the sound on discs and in the same year the first sound studio was built. Yet it was to be four years before Japan was to release its first sound-on-film talkie.

Many of the directors used the *Shomin-geki* as their starting point, but it is important to note that even at this early stage there were two distinct approaches to this form of middle-class realism, which was to emerge again after the war as the split between the ethical left and the ethical right. Politics were not really the motivating force at this time, the attack being rather against the corruption that appeared to be a permanent feature of the newly rich upper-middle-class. Mizoguchi developed his concern for the status of women in films such as *And yet they go on* (1931), a tale about women forced into prostitution. Yasujiro Ozu was still at this time making subtle middle-class comedies, in sharp contrast with the anti-capitalist polemics of many of his fellow directors. From this it can be seen that some directors were moving towards a position in which they showed life as it is, but made no comment or suggestion that it should be otherwise. Others showed life as it was but created characters who, either directly or certainly by inference, challenged the social status quo and dared to suggest directions of change.

One factor remains common in both styles of film, and is in direct contrast with Western cinema at this time. Because of their cultural heritage the Japanese are very susceptible to mood; much of the country's greatest art is solely for the creation of mood. The film-makers naturally built on this cultural core. By the time that the twenties were ending the best of the Japanese film-makers had realized that film must exist as film rather than as a second-hand form of theatre. From being at least fifteen years behind the rest of the world at the beginning of the decade they had caught up and even surpassed most other countries by the time that sound was married to the film. The concern with the realities of life had led the Japanese cinema to reject the 'well-made-play' format which still bedevils much of our cinema. They had successfully evolved an open, free-flowing style in which cinematic technique is used to express the emotional and intellectual content of the film. It does not become subservient to plot functions, as happened to many of the Hollywood products.

Whilst sound caused havoc in most other film industries the changes were few within the Japanese one. The *benshi* at last disappeared and were mourned by none, and some of the favourite stars suddenly became laughable once their voices could be heard and they quickly sank from view. A brief look at the first sound film will show how well sound suited the Japanese. *The*

The Neighbour's wife and mine (Gosho, Shochiku 1931)
A first essay in sound which proved the value of silence.

Neighbour's wife and mine directed by Gosho in 1931 was the first talkie and such was Gosho's awareness of the medium that he used as little dialogue as possible. This had two effects; firstly it allowed narrative to function at a much more economic level, by using just those words that were needed, and secondly the scarcity of the dialogue threw into sharp contrast the passages of non-verbal communication between the characters, at which the Japanese excel. Because of the written character of the Japanese language, in which a single word may have a number of meanings, they have a slight mistrust of the written word and an even greater mistrust of the spoken word since in speech there is no indication as to the meaning except the context.

It is noticeable that to this day the Japanese are often sparing in their use of dialogue, and perhaps as a result of caring more for the visual than the verbal have a fairly low standard of post-synchronization. In this first sound film Gosho used sound in a most inventive way, employing telling silences and using sounds from off-screen actions to create a larger sense of reality.

Sound brought a new vitality and joy to the screen; the films grew less tragic and dark, but the threads of social protest were not lost. The silent film was bound to die, but it is to the betterment of cinema that one of its last dying spasms was a masterpiece by anyone's standards. *I was born, but . . .*, made in 1932 by Ozu, the story of the two small sons of a clerk who is humiliated by his boss, the father of their friend, has a freshness which survives untarnished in our modern world. Brilliantly comic, the acting by the two

19

I was born but . . . (Ozu, Shochiku 1932)
The Keaton-like genius of children becomes a weapon of social comment.

boys owes a great deal to the films of Buster Keaton who was a top box-
office attraction in Japan. Ozu uses comedy and the innocence of children to
point to the inequalities of life. His children will grow up to be the same as the
father although they cannot at that age understand his behaviour. Ozu does
not, however, make a great protest about this; his film, full of all the technical
devices which he was later to reject, simply states that 'life is like that' and
there is little that can be done to change it.

With a genuine masterpiece as the first sound film and another as one of
the last silents the Japanese cinema made a smooth transition into the modern
age of the movie.

3 Sound and fury

Medieval Scene

Eleven warriors
Do not even turn their heads
Through the wind-blown snow.

Masaoko Shiki 1867–1902

The next ten years were to take Japan into a period of war. By 1930, militarism permeated the whole of Japanese society. It was therefore inevitable that this should affect and be displayed by the cinema industry. Within the physical laws of our world we accept that with action there is always reaction; in this country of the living paradox the cinema was both the natural instrument of nationalistic propaganda and at the same time the instrument for the human reaction to what was happening within society.

The militarism that had been the dominant feature of the social superstructures in previous centuries had been subdued towards the middle of the nineteenth century and its revival came from a surprising source. A certain Count Ito on a visit to Germany was instructed by Bismark in the ways of bonding a state together into a powerful unit capable of aggression. Bismark had had the task of unifying a number of states and then creating a form of Emperor. For the Japanese, on the other hand, the task was easier since they already had a tradition of the divinity of the Emperor. Bismark therefore suggested to Ito that he revive those parts of Shinto which exalt the authority and divinity of the Emperor.

Shinto, a basically tolerant and pantheistic religion, was carefully scrutinized and when found wanting was supplemented by bits of Confucianism and Christianity in order to create a 'New Shinto'. The priests were given greater powers, being granted the rights of burial and marriage, so they subtly increased their influence within the life of the people. Gradually new laws were made requiring the Shinto priest to officiate at many ceremonies. In this way Shinto became an instrument of the State and the practices of the faith a powerful force bonding the people. Ritual that featured the deity of the Emperor was increased and any opportunity to create a nationalistic feeling was seized upon and amplified. Schools were the most effective breeding-ground for new attitudes, and the ritual of Emperor worship in them reached such huge proportions that a Headmaster could lose his job and even his life if he made a mess of the ceremony of revealing the Emperor's portrait to the whole school – who were all bowing so low that they couldn't see it. However ludicrous this might seem to the cynical occidental the effect was immensely powerful and many reports speak of adults and children in tears of joy on such occasions.

Yojimbo (Kurosawa, Toho/Kurosawa Films 1961)
Mifune, as the archetypal silent hero, looks down on lesser mortals.

The intense patriotism generated by this process was later to be given a new direction by the military forces when patriotism was changed to xenophobia. A great deal is heard about the part that the samurai code of *bushido* played in the fighting prowess and the cruelty of the Japanese troops, but this is to do an injustice to *bushido* and to ignore the fanatical devotion which existed in the Japanese at this time. It is true that the military ideals were to some extent built upon the samurai's code of honour, but the elements were very carefully selected and mainly concentrated on those parts which stressed the need for sacrifice of one's self for the honour and glory of one's cause, which in this case was the Emperor and the Nation.

How did all this affect the film-makers, for they could not avoid involvement in such a massive cultural change?

Sound had arrived, and with it the cinema had found a new sense of reality.

Within a given context of a familiar world which now sounded, as well as looked real, directors could afford to sacrifice plot to character (rather than the other way round which is so often the mark of the majority of the films of the western world), the total effect of the film being derived from accumulative character studies.

This 'reality' and the willingness of the audience to accept it meant that much of the old style theatrical period pieces were now impossible. The hero now had a voice and had to be credible. He must either be silent in order to retain his mystery, for if we hear him too much we will notice his flaws, or he can reveal all his flaws to help us understand him as a human being. Many of the Japanese directors in the early years of sound used the period film as a vehicle for statement about the present day. In this they had a number of advantages over other countries. Many of the elements of the past still persisted in the social habits of the present, and whilst the audiences were generally quick to see the relevance of such films they could always be enjoyed for their surface value and were less likely to be struck by the growing government censorship.

In the two fields of the *Shomin-geki* and the period film the concern with character and especially with the individuality of a character can be seen as a reaction to the growth of the military powers. The new conditioning was towards subjugation of the individual to the group, especially the family unit which was now being glorified as analogous to the strength and security of the nation. The Tokogawa period had maintained its feudalism by keeping 'we' as the prime mode of thought. Literature in the first person had only just begun to emerge in the Showa period in the form of the *shishosetsu* novel, which was becoming a vastly popular genre, but there are many Japanese who felt that it had not yet reached any real maturity. For a people who for the most part have not been used to thinking of themselves as free individuals it has been difficult to raise this literary form much above the 'confessional' novel. It therefore tends to be rather shallow and slight; certainly there has been nothing in the *shishosetsu* to rival the great books of western literature, with their psychological depth. The Japanese have no indigenous Proust. Whilst these novels are slight they do provide good material for the cinema. The film is admirably suited to showing the surface reality of life and as a result many *shishosetsu* novels were rapidly translated into film. The novel of the inner man, the work of deeper psychology, presents almost insurmountable problems for the film director and has rarely been tackled by the Japanese.

The thirties then saw a number of pressures at work: the growth of the *Shomin-geki*, the increased search for reality, the use of the period film in an allegorical manner, and the growing nationalism and military pressure. The course of the cinema through this period can be marked by certain key examples.

Under the threat of war many of the directors felt there were personal aspects of life worth saving. At first they tended towards nostalgia, as in Heinosuke Gosho's *The Izu dancers* (1933) from the novel by the Nobel Prize winner Yasunari Kawabata, but very soon the weakness of nostalgia modulated into the almost plotless style of films such as Ozu's *Duckweed story* (1934) and Mizoguchi's *Osaka elegy* (1936). In the same year Mizoguchi made *Sisters of the Gion*, a story of two sisters, one a Geisha and the other in training, yet they are centuries apart in their attitudes. Here are all the elements of melodrama and tragedy, both of which are scrupulously avoided in this brilliant delineation of character.

These plotless films were very well received by an audience who were more interested in the humanity of the characters than the plot. In fact it

Sisters of the Gion (Mizoguchi, Nikkatsu 1936)
The conflict between the traditional and the modern which has tormented Japan for generations.

never occurred to the audience to look for a story, and 'plot-consciousness' only occurred to critics after the war-time propagandists had insisted on narrative movies.

The element of paradox that one finds so often in things Japanese shows strongly in the period films that were being made in the late thirties. At a time when the Japanese armies were crashing remorselessly through Manchuria and then China, and the military fanaticism was gripping the home front, the period film depicting war in feudal times, filled with just those people who lived by the *bushido* codes that were then being lauded, had become anti-feudal, almost anti-military. The heroes, rather than being supermen, were full of human virtues and vices.

In the same year (1937) as the rape of Nanking, one of the most important makers of period films, Sadao Yamanaka, made his greatest film. He recreated the total texture and feel of the Tokogawa period, not according to traditional literature as an age of princes, lords and samurai, but as an age of simple people, honest and dishonest, strong and weak. Most of all he attempted to explore those human values which are common to all periods. In his last and most important film *Humanity and paper balloons* he told the tale of a samurai who, through poverty, had been forced to sell his swords in order to buy rice. As if this were not enough degradation for a samurai his wife had to work, making paper balloons. From this situation the fates are so much against the samurai that his death is inevitable. The film itself uses the low camera position that was to become the stylistic mark of Ozu. The antecedents of such a style, which is of particular importance in cinematic history, might be found in the framings of the classical theatre or in the compositions of the screen paintings. Yamanaka used deep-focus to edit in depth, to create frame dynamics and relationship between characters, rather than use the techniques of cutting. Many directors of silent films had used this technique, though few as well as Yamanaka. (The combined talents of Orson Welles and Greg Toland are sometimes credited with the discovery of editing in depth – the use of new film stocks in *Citizen Kane* together with brilliant creative imagination certainly led to the finest example of this style.) The intense humanity of Yamanaka's films marks him out as the founder of a humanistic line that reaches on through Kurosawa, Ichikawa and Kobayashi. Shortly after completing this film he was sent to the war in China as an ordinary soldier where he died. Yamanaka's use of past cultures as a structure within which to make his statements is much stronger in effect than the use of the Western myth as a genre framework since the people themselves, the audiences, feel themselves to be very close to the past, more so even than the Americans do to their cowboy frontiersmen. The past permeates the present to a remarkable degree even in today's Japan.

As the second Sino–Japanese war increased in intensity and the state increased its pressure on the film industry to propagate those values which subjugated the individual to the demands of the nation, there were, as has been noted, major movements in the other direction, namely an increase in the humanist element, especially within the two genres of the *Shomin-geki* and the period film.

Like most other peoples in the world the Japanese are sentimental about children. During this difficult period several directors made films about children, seizing the chance to use the child's viewpoint to make comment on the adults through the eyes of innocence. No genre can suddenly appear as a full-grown individual and the child picture was no exception. Ozu had already given his damning, but dazzlingly funny, view of the materialistic adult world in *I was born, but . . .* in 1932, and now directors such as Tasaka, Yamamoto

A Pebble by the roadside (Tasaka, Nikkatsu 1938)
A humanist plea for the individual in the face of prewar militarism.

and Toyoda laid the solid foundation for a genre of films that have been consistently popular to the present day.

In the following year Tasaka came under the direction of the Department of Propaganda, yet once again he managed to blend his theme of humanism with another, apparently contradictory genre, the war film. *Five scouts* (1939) would have been an outstanding film under any circumstances, but at the time of filming the Ministry of Propaganda were demanding films which displayed the virtue of group unity. In response to this Tasaka produced a story of five individuals, each of them superbly delineated and set in totally convincing circumstances. Worst of all, as far as the Ministry were concerned, the film had no real plot, for its story of a reconnaissance patrol and its delayed return is much less important than the people themselves and the military structure within which they operate. At the end of the film, the five men are seen going back into battle – an indictment of the inhumanity of the military clique that sends men to die.

In terms of cinematic skill the film is quite stunning, from the rapid tracking shots under the titles to the still *contre-jour* ending of the gates through which the soldiers have marched. The camera movement and the control of the lighting to produce dynamic framing have doubtless given subsequent film-makers an example which has rarely been equalled. Early in the film as the five volunteer scouts leave the camp there is a sequence in which the camera tracks with the closely grouped running soldiers. Starting at grass level the camera rises slowly over a distance of about a quarter of a mile to perhaps fifteen feet high. Suddenly this cuts to a hand-held shot as the soldiers run along a water-filled drainage ditch. The fluidity of this movement

Five scouts (Tasaka, Nikkatsu 1938)
The use of dynamic framing in a powerfully human piece of intended propaganda.

Mud and soldiers (Tasaka, Nikkatsu 1939)
Using a loose formal structure Tasaka made an anti-military statement with all the panache of a military epic.

does not strike the viewer as simple virtuosity but grows organically from the action. The photography has a superb quality, the light reflecting off the edges of the characters and the camera free and flowing. The night scenes in the camp are structured in a quiet way with long pauses in conversations and small bursts of activity. This makes the grand imperial messages seem strangely out of place and somewhat irrelevant. The total mise-en-scène is very 'real' in terms of the space and activity of military life and when the enemy are encountered they are in no way personalized – it is a film about all wars and has affinities to the apocalyptic vision at the end of *Hell is for heroes* and the human interaction in *Westfront 1918* and *All quiet on the Western front*.

In the night scenes the use of shadows to create dynamic framing is bold but never obtrusive: great shadows break vast areas of the screen adding brilliant new compositions and presage the use of the wide screen.

After the scouts have returned one of them starts to sing the national song; slowly the others join in and in his room the commander stands to attention. One man's need for personal strength and comfort gives unity to a larger group of men. An added theatricality is given to the commander's final speech by the orchestration of gunfire in the background acting like the blocks and gongs of Noh music.

Humanist/military films continued to be made throughout the war, although it became increasingly difficult for any director to make a statement that did not conform to the wishes of the Ministry of Propaganda. Tasaka made what was perhaps the last overt statement with *Mud and soldiers* (1939). Here he used the story structure of a long, seemingly endless march, during which a number of incidents take place. Such a film might be expected from a defeated nation, but not from one in the middle of a great conquest. The following year Kozaburo Yoshimura attempted to express some of these

The Last days of Edo (Inagaki, Nikkatsu 1941)
The period film as a vehicle for Government propaganda.

ideals about the individuality of man in *The Story of tank commander Nishizumi* (1940) by showing the soldier as a compassionate and liberal individual. Yoshimura tried to suggest that there was no division between the officers and the ordinary ranks, a state which rarely existed in an army in which the officers were still mainly samurai. This film caused some trouble with the authorities but it was released. Occasionally the ministry used the period film to put over its propaganda message, such as Inagaki's *The Last days of Edo* (1941) but those directors who had developed the period film as an individual statement were actively discouraged from continuing unless they were prepared to make films strictly to order, either for the Ministry of Propaganda or for the Home Office.

Once the Pacific campaign had escalated and Japan joined battle with the United States and the Allies, there was an increased need for propaganda films. A selection of titles alone will indicate the type of film: *Flaming sky, Towards the decisive battle in the sky, Navy, Generals, staff and soldiers, The Suicide troops of the watch tower, The War at sea from Hawaii to Malaya* and so on through a catalogue of ultra-nationalism. In addition to overt military propaganda there were a large number of films about the war but not about the soldiers. They were simple stories of simple heroism by nurses, interpreters and the parents on the home-front all making their sacrifices for the good of the country and the glory of the Emperor. Few of these films really managed to explore character, but were content to use people as ciphers to serve greater purposes. This is not however to say that these films were not well made, since the Japanese directors knew their American cinema, and, ironically, in order to make war films of the 'well-made' type they did not hesitate to imitate those of the enemy.

From 1942 to the end of the war there was a marked increase in the use of the documentary techniques that had been evolving over the preceding five years. In order to show the people on the home-front the progress that was being made feature-length documentaries were compiled from newsreel footage. Such material can very easily be biased, and many of the Tokyo studios developed such sophisticated techniques of studio shooting that the results were indistinguishable from the actuality footage: after the defeat of Japan the American forces impounded a great deal of studio footage thinking it was genuine record material of the war. The lessons learned here were not lost and there are many fine examples of high quality model work to be found in some recent Japanese films, not least in the animation of monsters.

The story of the films not directly concerned with the military conduct of the war is complex. The influence of the authorities was everywhere. Directives from above forced directors to give films a happy ending (not so common in the Japanese film), and they had to stress the theme of duty, duty to one's family and to the nation. Toyoda even made a film *A Record of my love* (1941) urging unmarried women to marry disabled soldiers, both as a duty to the nation and also to relieve the state of its financial responsibility; and this was from the man who had made *Spring on leper's island* (1940), an individual and compassionate plea in the middle of a war.

There were exceptions to this capitulation. Gosho with his great mastery of the *Shomin-geki* managed to turn nearly every script that he was given into a clear and simple story about complex and utterly real people, with very little reference to the war. Mizoguchi attempted to avoid complicity in the propaganda by retreating into history. From the Meiji period he made superb character studies in *The Story of the last chrysanthemums* (1939) and *Woman of Osaka* (1940). But even he was forced by the authorities to retreat even further into the Tokogawa period and make a version of the *Loyal forty-seven Ronin of the Genroku era* (1941). This was supposed to inspire the war effort, but it did not do so as he turned it into a sombre elegy for the dead.

Generals, staff and soldiers (Taguchi, Musei Eiga Kanshokai 1942)
Like all the other combatants Japan used the war film to stir the national pride.

The Earth (Uchida, Nikkatsu 1939)
The 'documentary' feature which examined the very texture of life; reality reflected by the textures of the earth.

It was during these years of conflict that the documentary was raised to a creative art, not only as a means of structured reportage, but also as a means of constructing a human statement. *Earth* (1939) by Tomu Uchida was filmed as a documentary, although it had a fine structure imposed by the director. In order to observe peasants in their daily life throughout the changing seasons the film was shot during one year on a farm. The observation of character is immaculate and the texture of the rural life is almost perfect. The film has an underlying ambiguity, for to show life as it is, to observe the bad and the good together is to make an intrinsic criticism of those aspects of life that one has shown. Japan never really had the sort of documentary group such as the one that surrounded John Grierson in Britain, but the documentary tradition, as exemplified in *Earth*, has been one into which a director of feature films can move with ease. Documentaries are still regarded as honourable companions to feature films, possibly because of the war-time habit of coupling a documentary with a feature when the government banned the issue of double-bill programmes.

Following the success of *Earth*, the same formula was tried with less success by Kajiro Yamamoto when he made the film *Horse*. This film has possibly attracted more critical attention than it really deserves, since it is known that parts of the film were directed by Yamamoto's assistant, Akira Kurosawa. Some critics have played the game of trying to work out which bits were made by Kurosawa, an activity which seems to be of little value compared with a study of his first film made shortly after the completion of *Horse*. *Sanshiro sugata* (*The Judo story*, 1943) marked the emergence of a major talent. This story of the conflict between judo and jujitsu as exemplified in the young hero, would have been remarkable at any time, but as a first directorial effort in 1943 it is even more noteworthy. At a time when there were strict controls Kurosawa managed to make a film which was read by the authorities as an extolling of the national virtues but which on closer examination is a strongly individual plea for the humanist values. Following this he returned to the documentary style to make *The Most beautiful* (1944) about girls working in a factory, and then, under a certain amount of pressure from the Ministry of Propaganda, he made *Sanshiro sugata II*. Perhaps as a result of the complete nature of the statement in the first film with its delicate balance of opposing forces, both natural and human, this second version lacks some of the sincerity of the original and is not held in high regard by Kurosawa himself. As the war came to an end he adapted the Kabuki stage to the screen with his personal version of *Kanjincho* as the film *Tora no o fumu kotachi* (*They who step on a tiger's tail*, 1945), one of the first casualties of Occupation censorship.

The other major movement that was to emerge from the war and continue after it can be attributed to one man, Yasujiro Ozu. Undoubtedly one of the greatest directors of the Japanese cinema, and surely one of the great masters of the film medium throughout the world, Ozu was beginning his stunning document on the complex nature of the Japanese people; his characters are supremely Japanese but not uniquely so since Ozu has managed to make one of the greatest universal statements on the nature of man through his films. At no time was he really diverted from his course as Japan rose to be a major military power, fought a cataclysmic war and was eventually crushed into ignominious defeat.

4 Industry reformed

Spring Rain

Spring rain:
And the frogs bellies
Are not yet wet.

Taniguchi Buson 1715–1783

The Second World War ended in effect for Japan at the instant of the atomic blast in Peace Square. What happened in Japan after the surrender and through the Occupation is a strange and confusing tale, no matter what aspect of life one wishes to consider. One cannot totally separate out the film industry and say that the people within it behaved in a strange way, since they were all part of the same defeated people. None of the member nations amongst the Allies has ever had the experience of crashing from centuries of self-sufficiency and glory in conquest to a terrible defeat and subjugation, and it is all too easy for outsiders to criticize the actions of many Japanese. Within the film industry alone there were many who performed a triple *volte-face* in the air without the aid of a net, and enough coats were turned to keep a nation of tailors happy. But this is to make a cheap joke of people who had suddenly to adjust from praising an Emperor and purveying the nationalistic propaganda to some strange ideas of democracy that were dictated by the new military overlords. The paradox of Japan has even affected the situation of the Occupation; for MacArthur, in attempting to rid Japan of centuries of feudal tradition, especially that of the Shogun and the samurai clans, took upon himself a role which was almost exactly that of the Shogun. The Japanese knew exactly what he was doing even if they did not at first know how to cope with his ideas.

But what of the film industry under these new circumstances? In the intensive bombing nearly half of the cinemas had been destroyed, but miraculously the studios were hardly touched, allowing the industry to continue almost unbroken as far as production was concerned. This left the minor problem of distribution and the major problem of the Occupation forces. In October of 1945 there were 845 cinemas but by January of 1946 there were 1,137 and this rate of building continued for some time. One of the factors in this increase was that they were considered to be a good investment. Perhaps because of this a number of the criminal fraternity became heavy backers of the buildings if not of actual film production.

The problem that really faced the industry was the new direction in which it was being steered by the Occupation forces of General MacArthur, or SCAP as it was known, for the Americans reacted to the fierce nationalism of war-time by imposing very strict censorship. There were 554 films made during the war that were reviewed by SCAP and of these 225 were considered feudal or anti-democratic and were to be destroyed. Because these films had already been distributed around the country SCAP could never be certain that they had all the prints and negatives and it is fortunate for us that they weren't too efficient. Amongst those films that they tried to destroy were Tasaka's *Five scouts*, Inagaki's *Musashi miyamoto* (1940) and Kurosawa's films *Sanshiro sugata* and *They who step on a tiger's tail*. (The latter they banned because of what they saw as feudal remnants.)

SCAP not only reviewed all the old films but took control of scripts. It took many months for them even to formulate any policy and it is reported that on location the cry of 'Wait for the sun to come out' was changed to 'Wait for the Occupation Army to make up its mind'. The SCAP office did however get rid of many of the restrictions which had been placed by the war-time government. They freed film-making from being the property of just one company, and the executives returned to their own offices.

But woe betide anyone who went against SCAP, or worse still ignored them. Ichikawa had his puppet film, *Girl at the Dojo temple* (1945–46), burned before it was even released simply because he had not submitted the script. To this day he solidly maintains that this was one of his best films.

SCAP formed a Civil Censorship Division and listed the types of film that were to be made in order to secure its objectives: 'that Japan will never in the future disturb the peace of the world. . . .' The restrictions included 'anything infused with militarism, revenge, nationalism, or antiforeignism; distortion

They who step on a tiger's tail (Kurosawa, Toho 1945)
The introduction of Enoken (left), as the kyogen character, to mock the worst elements of feudalism.

of history; approval of racial or religious discrimination; favouring or approving feudal loyalty or treating human life lightly; direct or indirect approval of suicide; approval of the oppression or degradation of wives; admiration of cruelty or unjust violence; anti-democratic opinion; exploitation of children; and any opposition to the Potsdam Declaration or any SCAP order.' Such restrictions have never been applied to the American cinema.

By March of 1946 the control of films had become the province of the Civil Information and Education (CI & E) Section of the Occupation and it was nearly four years before the Japanese gained control of their own industry.

As in all countries that have been defeated in war there comes a time, as that country is just beginning to get back on its feet, that people look around for somebody to blame for what has happened. Purges spread like a pernicious disease. The Japanese film industry set about naming its 'war criminals' and here demonstrated the most extreme contrasts. The CI & E turned to the Japan Motion Picture and Drama Employees Union and asked it to draw up its list of war criminals. What the Americans may have failed to notice was that this Union was a strong Communist clique. As could have been expected the naming of 'war criminals' was as much an act of political revenge as it was a passage of justice. Much bitterness has resulted from this act and as late as the last two years those who suffered from the 'list' have been fighting their cases.

Another strange fact about the list was that the Americans classified the 'criminals' as those who could never work in films again, those who would be suspended and those who would simply have to be watched very carefully. The initial list had too many people in each sector so the Japanese simply reduced the number of names, at which point many a director drew a heartfelt sigh of relief.

Before the war, industry had organized itself into a number of huge combines or *zaibatsu* which within the given structure made a lot of sense, yet when looked at from the viewpoint of democracy appeared suspect. What happened was that a large industry would take into the combine all those other companies that had anything to do with the manufacture of supplies or services to the major industry. In this way vast numbers of small companies would be placed under the paternal care of an immensely rich giant. SCAP charged in with its ideas of democracy based on Washington, and with little regard for the culture of the occupied people, and immediately broke up the giant *zaibatsu*, thereby 'freeing' the smaller companies. Initially the Japanese were as fanatical about democracy as they are about any new idea. This lasted less than two years when a slightly depressed stock market threw fear into most industrial hearts as the smaller companies found that they could no longer afford to go through a bad patch buoyed up by finance from the parent body. Now they had to maintain a strong face in the daily battle of the stock market. Consequently, once the Occupation forces left Japan, industry quickly and quietly set about re-establishing her *zaibatsu*. They are to a large degree responsible for the position that Japan holds in the world today – but it is doubtful if they would work in quite the same way in the rest of the world since they would lack that essential ingredient, the Japanese people.

In the context of this industrial structure it is easier to see why, during the war, the government had reduced the film industry to virtually one company: control was easier that way. Toho as the biggest producer of wartime films had come out on top and when SCAP reinstated the other companies Toho held the whip hand. But this was to be a bitter time for the industry. The major companies were fighting for the large slice of the cake that was the viewing public. The newly formed unions had seized on the ideas of 'democracy' and were led by people trained in Moscow and in the USA. Companies formed and split, actors and directors left to form their own groups only to be bought back at vast expense by the parent companies when they found themselves without any production talent. It was not until late in 1949 that some recognizable pattern emerged with the five major companies in a precarious state of balance.

But before it could achieve any sort of stability the industry had to go through what must be the most extraordinary battle that has ever been witnessed around a film studio. 1948 was the year of the strikes at Toho. The reasons for the troubles within the various companies are complex and have been well documented by Joseph Anderson and Donald Richie, and it is not the author's intention to repeat all the details here, but in an attempt to show how the industry developed towards its present position a few points will be helpful.

During 1947–8 Toho had three strikes. From the first two the unions gained pay rises and improved conditions together with a limited voice in the running of the company, but it seems to have been obvious to many that there were bigger things to come. Despite splinter unions forming and further complicating the issue the main union had many adherents who saw that this next strike, the third in Toho, would be a rehearsal for a general strike. There was an essential conflict between the workers and the management, many of whom had little or nothing to do with films, having come from industry. (It is interesting that a similar situation of industrial take-over of motion pictures was to take place much later in the USA.)

Taking note of the success of the railway workers' strike in which they had had a 'work in' and allowed passengers free travel, the film crews occupied the studios and kept out the management. This strike, seen by many at the time to be a heroic struggle, and naturally by others as national sabotage, lasted one hundred and ninety-eight days. During this time there were battles between rival unions and court orders which proved to be useless. Eventually the management went to the Tokyo police who later turned up with two thousand armed police. This seemingly huge army was reinforced by one company of cavalry, seven armoured cars together with tanks and three fighter planes, all from the US Eighth Army. Such force was first met with jeers and poetry from the strikers, but when the massed troops shaped up for the attack those inside soon negotiated a settlement. As the barricades were being removed the strikers emerged as a procession singing the 'Internationale' and carrying red banners. A splendidly theatrical gesture, but one which did nothing to prevent the sackings and purges that were to follow.

Toho had been near the edge of financial ruin because of the strikes. Shintoho had broken away from the larger Toho company and found themselves without the finance that was needed to get off the ground. Daiei had consistently made military films throughout the war and therefore had nothing that they could show, nothing with which they could build up a new circuit. The period films were tied up by Toho so they set out to make sensational pictures of sex and violence. Such subjects might be disparaged by today's reformers but they managed to make Daiei solvent. The jostling for position was to continue for the next few years. Foreign films were imported and in the main were successful, co-productions were tried and proved to be failures, the taxes on cinema admission prices rose from the wartime one hundred per cent to a world record of one hundred and fifty per cent. In order to cover the costs of film import and the rising costs of film production, including the buying in of much American equipment such as Mitchell cameras, admission prices rose to a level more than one hundred times that of the pre-war prices. Only the steady increase in attendance figures saved the industry at this point.

At the heads of most companies sat businessmen, accountants, and entre-preneurs rather than film-makers, and through their efforts the major companies returned to their monopolistic existence, controlling production, marketing and distribution. Smaller companies tended to disappear under pressure from the larger companies or were bought over. In 1961, eighteen companies were engaged in full time film production, but five companies accounted for nearly seventy-five per cent of production. The scale of operation can be judged from the figures. These had reached a peak in 1960 with a total of 547 feature films released, earning $202,000,000 in box office receipts.

The rise from the unrest of the late forties to this peak is quite remarkable but it was certainly not smooth running for all the companies. Shochiku went through a severe depression round about 1950 as a result of its policy of making films of a domestic comedy type. The Japanese audiences were tired of the genre and it was several years before Shochiku managed to find a viable substitute. Fortunately for them in the early sixties they began to make gangster films at just the right moment for the audiences and their fortunes rose once more.

Toho, the real giant of the industry, had even worse trouble, for after its strikes and a 1948 production record of only four feature films, they came even nearer to ruin in 1950 finding that they could not pay the required admission taxes, having used the money to pay staff wages. The Tokyo Metropolitan

Rashomon (Kurosawa, Daiei 1950)
Light gleaming on flesh in a film filled with unforgettable surfaces, whose truth and reality we are led to doubt.

Tax Office took action and got an order for the sale of four of the company's most lucrative Tokyo cinemas. Company officials literally went begging round the offices of their competitors. By the end of the week they had raised half the money and promised to pay the rest soon. As if this were not enough four of the best directors, Kurosawa, Yamamoto, Naruse and Taniguchi had left to form their own company. A few years later Toho payed out a fortune to buy this small company, The Motion Picture Art Association, a far from petty action since amongst the films that this group had produced was *Rashomon*.

The success of *Rashomon* prompted companies to make films for a foreign market, often by imitating the prize-winning films from other countries. They sincerely believed they could win foreign film festivals on the strength of the quality of the imitation. Others thought that since the foreigners knew nothing of Japan then the films should be disguised travelogues – these met with the same fate as the co-productions. Political alignment emerged amongst the companies, and the purged communists gathered in the Hokusei Motion Picture Company, which exists today as the Daito Motion Picture Company. Daito attempted to grab part of the cheap film market but were pushed out by Toei.

By the middle of 1952 the five major companies had achieved a rough state of balance. That year the Americans reduced the entertainment tax from one hundred and fifty per cent to a mere fifty per cent. However, the cost of admission did not fall, the companies pocketing the difference to help cover rising costs. For a while they were almost embarrassed by their wealth as the tax was further reduced to ten per cent. Everyone profited for a short time. Yet despite this Shintoho almost failed, for having worked out that they could make gangster and military films successful as long as they were right wing they still came near to being bankrupt. Eventually they sank everything into a widescreen production called *The Emperor Meiji and the great Russo–Japanese war* (1956). Despite being a very poor film it was a great success; it might have been that it was considered bad to criticize a film about an Emperor. More likely was the thrill of the new wide screen, although *The Robe* (1953) had been imported and had broken box-office records all over the country. Shintoho made two more expensive widescreen films about Emperors and found out to their cost that people could lose their fascination with a technical device. However this was not before some theatre owners had been found masking the top and bottom of standard ratio films and using a long screen. One owner even did that to an American 3-D picture.

From the October 1945 total of 845 cinemas numbers had risen to over 6,000 by January 1957 and building continued at the rate of two new cinemas opening somewhere every day. The film industry doubled in size that year and a sixth giant company appeared on the scene, Nikkatsu, which had previously been a commercial company owning cinemas. Even though there were three years to go to the production peak the companies now began to sow the seeds of their future difficulties. Most of them set up production schedules of one feature film per week and Toei even entered on a scheme of completing two full-length features per week, a rate which they managed to maintain for over five years. In order to capture audiences, every cinema began to run double-bill programmes. Toei controlled nearly one third of them, all showing exclusively Toei films. Under this sort of pressure such development could not be maintained, and inevitably once expansion faltered, recession set in.

The extent of this recession can be seen by considering the figures for 1960 and 1970, for the number of cinemas has fallen alarmingly from 7,457 to 3,246 in those ten years, and attendance has fallen from the record 1,014 million to a steadily reducing 253 million. The only hopeful figure is that of production which has only been reduced from 547 to 423 feature films a year, and still remains the highest single language national production figure in the world. The main reason for this fall can be attributed to the rapid growth of television which has mushroomed into a vast number of stations. This forced companies to rationalize production, but has helped the industry in a way since a great deal of production is now made specifically for the small screen. Whilst the major companies still hold sway there has been a rapid growth in recent years of small independent companies producing low-budget, less commercially orientated films. More than two hundred of these are registered in Tokyo alone.

Thus like the rest of Japanese industry the motion picture business has struggled through the trauma of defeat to a position of world power. It now reflects the malaise that is hitting the cinema industry in all other countries. By virtue of the volume alone one would expect that some of these films would be good – both from experience and from the reports of others we know full well that Japan has consistently produced films that can be considered alongside the best in the world. However, one does not have to be long in Japanese cinemas before one sees that the general standard is not the same as that of Ozu, Mizoguchi or Kurosawa, and it is noticeable that every year in the Kinema Jumpo 10 Best Awards (the equivalent of the American Oscars), at least six of the recognized nine best directors have been appearing for the last fifteen years.

Part two

Japanese cinema: an ethical spectrum

5 Post-war emergence

The myth is still perpetuated in the writings of many critics around the world that Japanese films suddenly broke through some invisible national barrier into a surprised world with the victory of *Rashomon* at the 1951 International Film Festival in Venice. Since that time the story has grown up that this particular film was unknown and unrecognized in its own country; one has even read in a highly respected film magazine that the Japanese found themselves without any copies when they realized that the film might have box-office value and had to re-import them from abroad. But one wonders from where they could have 're-imported' copies since being an unknown film it would hardly have been exported.

Neither story has any real foundation. It is true that the Japanese have always been, and to some extent still are, reticent about exposing their films to an occidental audience, but it would be wrong to think that nothing had been exported before *Rashomon*. Many films were distributed throughout the Orient and a limited number had found their way to the USA. In 1928 Japan had already scored a singular triumph with the distribution of *The Passion of a woman teacher* (1926) directed by Mizoguchi and *Crossways* (1928) by Kinugasa, which both had good reviews, especially from the German critics and film-makers. *Rashomon* was certainly the first major post-war success, but it has been by no means the only one. Contrary to the myth *Rashomon* had been a success at the box-office, and had in many ways become something of a cult. Europeans may at first have thought that this film was typical of the way in which Japanese narrative style attempted to explore the 'truth' of a situation. In fact it was just as much a puzzle to the Japanese audiences as it was to those in the West, perhaps more so, since its approach was diametrically opposed to the norm and the audiences sincerely believed that there must be a correct solution to the puzzle. Such an answer would have suited their well-ordered minds, which found it difficult to cope with a set of unresolved possibilities.

The award of the Grand Prix came as a surprise but it was certainly something on which the industry in general has attempted to capitalize. The search for a prize-winning formula turned out to be a failure, but nevertheless Japan has maintained a steady rate of international successes. That these do not always correspond to the awards issued in the Kinema Jumpo annual list of 10 best films says something about both the Western view of Japan and also the Japanese critics' view of indigenous film. It is sometimes obvious that there are different criteria in operation, and it is hoped that by a consideration of some of those aspects and qualities of life that have motivated the film-makers, the reader may be in a better position to balance his conditioned Occidental response to the films against a slight knowledge of some of the background within Japanese society and culture.

Since 1951 UniJapan, the association for the diffusion of Japanese films abroad, has consistently presented films in international festivals. To take a reasonably average year 1964 saw forty-one presentations with a return of eight prizes. 1967 was even more productive with the gaining of twenty overseas prizes through such films as *Red beard* (Kurosawa), *Kwaidan* (Kobayashi), *Onibaba* (Shindo) and *Tokyo Olympiad* (Ichikawa). These directors are now of world renown, but it is more than a little sad that there are directors of near or equal talent whose work has hardly ever been seen in the cinemas of Europe or America. Few cineastes have had the opportunity of viewing the works of Naruse, Gosho, Imai, Kinugasa, Ito and many others.

6 Ethical left, ethical right

Waiting

A man, just one–
A fly, just one–
In the large guest room.

Issa 1762–1826

It is only a hundred years since Japan ceased to be a police state, and much less than that since the apparent removal of the 'feudal remnants'. For a people with as long a history as the Japanese this is little more than the passing of a night. It is true that since that time they have been ravaged by war and were for a time an occupied and oppressed people; it is equally true that the influences of the rest of the world, particularly the cultural values of the USA are gnawing steadily at the very heart of the nation – yet despite all these pressures the past still threads its way throughout Japanese life and binds it all together. For the Japanese the past is very real, so that, by the integration of past customs into the country's religions and many of the living habits of modern technological society, a strange co-existence of ancient and modern has been established, a living set of contradictions, an active paradox.

The life of the ordinary Japanese, especially those of the middle class, is still very much governed by traditions; regulations, albeit unwritten, still act as the touchstone for action. Loyalty to the group, be it family, factory or gang, is still the predominant influence – especially now that loyalty to a nationalistic creed has been virtually submerged. It is not yet the norm for a Japanese to act as a complete individual, and he tends to feel insecure under these circumstances. A Japanese professor recently stated that the differences between Japanese and Occidental societies lay in the fact that the Occidental has the conditioning which enables him to weigh up a set of circumstances and rationally work out his subsequent course of action, the individuality of this action being its most important aspect, whereas the Japanese does not have the facility to do this, tending to act within a corporate structure or group and even then operating by a predetermined pattern.

Such a gross simplification would lead one to expect Japan to be full of automata acting within the confines of some unwritten programme. Reality is very different from this arid image; the Japanese being as alike and unalike each other as most other peoples. Yet there is much truth in what was said of them. The need to exist as part of a group or within a set family pattern is very strong. It can be seen in the readiness with which the ordinary Japanese are prepared to give themselves to the paternal care of a large industrial combine.

Devotion on the railway (Sekigawa, PCL 1960)
A modern and somewhat melodramatic version of the clash between love and duty.

The existence of the group identity is strongly displayed in the behaviour of the Japanese student whether he is rioting or attending classes. Such is the extent of this desire for group identity that school children and students wear uniforms that are virtually indistinguishable no matter what college or area. One feels that it almost amounts to a fear of being singled out as an individual.

With this in mind it is interesting to find that within the Japanese film industry, especially since the last war, there has been a definite group of film-makers who plead strongly for the right of an individual to exist as a separate and free entity. However, that these films can be seen as a definite group depends on understanding what they are reacting against. It is therefore necessary to look at those films which represent the traditional world-picture the Japanese have of themselves, the conservative view, in order that we might better examine the other extreme. To clarify this distinction it is useful to refer to the traditionalists as the ethical right wing and the protesters as the ethical left. It must be stressed at this point that this has little direct correlation to a political left/right polarization, although as will be seen there is an occasional tendency towards such an alignment.

Donald Richie has written: 'Of all the Japanese directors, only Kurosawa and Ozu have taken the particular difficulties of being Japanese and enlarged them to include the truly international difficulty of being at all'. In the final analysis one feels that this statement is true, but it contains the whole of the problem of the two divergent movements within the Japanese film. How can it be that these two directors manage to produce films which have the same powerful universal quality when they are diametrically opposed in their attitudes and their modes of expression?

Ozu possibly comes closest to defining the essentially Japanese way of life. With his observation of the unfriendly ordinary world he attempts to recognize man's inner self with all its limitations, trying to live in harmony with himself and the world by refusing to trespass, by refusing conflict, by accepting the chaos and the injustice, by realizing that all things pass and that the self changes just as much as the world does. This quality of human thought and existence which is so quintessentially Japanese is known as *mono-no-aware*. The total work of Ozu and many other post-war directors is infused with this quality. To call it fatalism would be to harden and falsify it to the mind of the occidental. There can be no direct translation of the term, it is much more complex and sophisticated than saying simply 'That's life. Tough isn't it?' Nor is it passive acceptance of a state of sadness. Perhaps *lacrimae rerum* comes closer than most towards a translation. If there is no parallel phrase in the English language the term can be made clearer by saying that it is that attitude of mind which knows that the way things happen is the way things must happen – not because any fates have dictated that it shall be so but because that is the natural order of the world.

Kurosawa rages through his films against what appears to be the natural order, even to the extent in *Rashomon* of denying the surface reality of human experience. The traditionalist states that things are as they seem to be; those at the other extreme shout that nothing is totally what it appears to be and that the individual can do more than simply exist within the observable world – he has a power to change it.

If we are to line up the protagonists in this philosophical battle of the left against the right the teams would be led by a major group on each side. On the right appear Ozu, Mizoguchi, Naruse and Gosho, whilst on the left in noisy contrast stand Kurosawa, Ichikawa and Kobayashi. Just looking at the products of these fine directors one can see the obvious contrast, but just as the surface has been shown to be false in *Rashomon* and as Gosho's *Where chimneys are seen* (1953) shows that there are always several viewpoints on any question, we must beware of too simplistic a division.

Ozu, Gosho, Naruse and Mizoguchi all made the majority of their films within the genre of *Shomin-geki*, middle class realism. All their films demonstrate in one way the nature of *mono-no-aware*. In the films of Ozu not only the characters but the whole form of the film embodies this attitude, whilst in contrast the world of Mizoguchi, though full of characters who live in accordance with such a mode, is by implication a criticism of many of the attitudes which the ordinary Japanese hold as their main guide-lines.

Within this group, whose films share a certain similarity of mood, there are important differences. This may have arisen from the way in which the Japanese film has been divided and subdivided into 'tendencies'. Whether this is another manifestation of the Japanese desire for predetermined sets or not is hard to discover, but it is noticeable that production is sectionalized into 'mother films' or *haha-mono*, the *tsuma-mono* or 'wife films' and so on, with rules as to what is and is not done to or by the central character in each *mono*. There are even *monro-mono* for the type of film in which Marilyn Monroe appeared. Harold Lloyd also fathered a *mono* and the glasses he wore are still refered to as *roido*. There are therefore a number of distinct subdivisions within the general field of 'domestic' or 'home' films.

Period films are also the forte of Kurosawa and Kobayashi, though they

Where chimneys are seen (Gosho, Studio Eight 1953)
Gosho's meticulous and sympathetic examination of life from different view-points. Near-perfect middle-class realism.

both use contemporary settings as well. It is perhaps unfortunate that we in the west have been exposed mainly to the period work of both these directors, since their modern films are equally as good and demonstrate fully the consistency of thought which pervades all their work. Also, it is by this very consistency that we are able to classify these directors.

On the one hand we have characters who accept life, those who fail, those who become resigned to the status quo; such are the figures of Ozu – the parents in *Tokyo Story* who learn to accept the bitter disappointment of their dashed hopes for their children, contrasted with the inner beauty of the daughter-in-law who has come to terms with her lot without losing her compassion and understanding; such are the figures of Naruse who find their only answer in ultimate defeat and death; such are the figures of Mizoguchi, men who find lives made whole by the love of a woman, and women who find life losing its meaning without the love of a man.

On the other hand there are the protesters, the determined individuals. Since this is a more modern concept such figures tend to portray modern thought within a classical setting. Such men are the wandering samurai of *Yojimbo* and *Sanjuro* from Kurosawa or Kobayashi's father figures in *Harakiri* and *Rebellion*. They find direct parallels in the actions, no less heroic, of the dying civil servant in *Ikiru* as he slices through the bureaucratic morass, and the magnificent characters from Ichikawa – the dedicated monk in *The Burmese harp*, the soldier in *Fires on the plain*, the lonely student talking to himself as he sails across a vast ocean in *Alone on the Pacific* and the *onnagata* with a single purpose in *An Actor's revenge*. The difference between these two camps might seem to be that between those who support the status quo and those who protest against it and that would mean that one had made an equation between protest and social consciousness. Yet films can be made in which the characters exemplify completely *mono-no-aware* and yet be implicit criticisms of the status quo, and at the other extreme a number of films have been made which had an overt intention of being critical towards the accepted social mores yet ended by supporting them.

For the Japanese, social consciousness is a relatively new phenomenon, having only really developed since the last war. Until recently the social order had created a duality of rules governing private and public life, resulting in dichotomies that are difficult to understand within a European code of social conduct. Films setting out to be overtly critical of the social system, such as *A Town of love and hate* (1959) by Nagisa Oshima, end by being superficial, largely because the questions they raise do not impinge on the generally held attitudes of the people. Criticism of the social order can be

When a woman loves (Gosho, Daiei 1960)
Gosho's social realism, particularly in regard to the place of women within society, is a clear statement of traditional values.

made very powerful, however, if firmly rooted in the reality of Japanese life.

Such a way is chosen by directors such as Kurosawa, the framework for whose statements has an impeccable texture of the real world in which characters can challenge the accepted order, and by others such as Mizoguchi who make the simple statement of that social reality a criticism in itself.

Although the methods of implicit statement that have been developed partly as a counter to the failure of overt criticism play a large part in any study of the Japanese cinema one must not imagine that Japanese films are solely of a critical nature. Such films are small in number if important in terms of cinematic art. The Japanese film tends to comment by reflecting the empirical reality of a situation rather than to criticize it, and as a result of this they have the enviable ability to devote equal strength and skill to the portrayal of the good side of life as well as the bad. This is what Donald Richie has called the ability to 'celebrate' life, and as he points out films of protest are usually strong in the West whilst films of celebration are weak. 'Celebration' need not entail a 'happy' story, and by considering firstly those films that have come from what we have termed the ethical right wing, it can be seen that through the medium of the motion picture a director, especially one of the calibre of Ozu, can celebrate a quality of life, *mono-no-aware*, with all its joy and sadness that is central to the very state of being Japanese.

7 Ozu: the quiet tradition

Basho's Road

This road:
No person going on it,
Autumn nightfall.

Matsuo Basho 1644–1694

To examine any one sector of a nation's cinema and to discover those things which characterize identifiable groups of films leads one first to an isolation of the various genres and then inevitably to a study of the work of particular directors. Whilst the *auteur* theory can prove a fruitful method of analysis of the greatest of the world's film directors, it is not the intention of this work to become involved in a series of analytical studies of the complete works of any particular director. Within each rough grouping there will be those who emerge as its finest exponents, and a lateral view through the work of a number of these directors, rather than a vertical study through a man's *œuvre* serves to demonstrate those basic elements that are the mark of a particular cinematic tendency.

Thus the ethical right wing of the Japanese cinema rests not in the work of a single director but in a group. Nor is it possible to delineate a single genre which will fully cover all the right wing attitudes. The largest part is contained within the *Shomin-geki*. To take a behaviourist point of view, a social characteristic of this mode of life is demonstrated by the actions of the subjects. Here one of the many paradoxes in Japan emerges. The action that most characterizes the traditional middle class is the *lack* of action, the unwillingness to take decisions, and a ready acceptance of the order of things without any effort to change them. This must not be judged as culpable negligence as it would be in terms of European socio-moral attitudes, but as a genuine method of transcending the troubles of this world, a difficult thing to achieve. This acceptance of the world and learning to come to terms with it is central both in *mono-no-aware* and to the films of Yasujiro Ozu.

From the earliest comedies one can see in the work of Ozu an increasing concern with this quality of life and thought. In order to concentrate on human attitudes Ozu has gradually shed all the elements of the normal narrative leaving only the people to interact. With *I was born, but ...* and *Chorus of Tokyo*, Ozu began to simplify the plots of his films. These two films have a linear structure with a few peaks of action and decision by the central characters; they also contain the theme of the very young teaching the older generation the error of their ways. This latter theme is reworked in *Passing fancy* (1933) but here the plot is lighter and the real point of individual decision only occurs near the end of the film. Once he had moved into the sound film Ozu had refined his style to the extent that one can see *The Only son* (1936) as the starting point for a long series of films about family life, all of which are characterized by the slightness of the plot – the positive rejection of anything that might be considered melodramatic. These films have an extraordinary vitality and tension for they are full of the potential for what we consider to be 'dramatic'. The 'action' takes place in the spaces between people, in the minutiae of behaviour and the conflict of attitudes, often unspoken.

Failure in the sense of unfulfilled aspirations is not regarded as something reprehensible by those Japanese who hold the views of the ethical right wing; by its very nature it has a certain kind of beauty. To many Japanese the festivals of the cherry blossom, when even the centres of the dirtiest cities are all but drowned in a sea of pink bloom, only reach their peak at the moment just before the blossoms die and fall. This moment of passing, a demonstration of the impermanence of life, echoes those human moments when hopes and dreams fall and die.

Chorus of Tokyo (1931) though showing some echoes of Lubitsch and Keaton has many of the elements of failed hope. The father, having lost his job with an insurance company for having dared to question the boss on behalf of another colleague, meets his former teacher who is now running a small restaurant. The sense of disappointment at seeing a man of former importance so low in the social scale is barely disguised, but out of loyalty to his former instructor the father agrees to carry a banner in the street advertising the noodle restaurant. In his turn he is a cause for disappointment in his wife who sees him parading with his banner. It is at this point that Ozu states the simple core of truth in the film when the father quietly defends his action to his wife with the words: 'Man is liable to depend on things that shouldn't be depended upon when he is hard up.'

This quality, that there are *lacrimae rerum* in our human struggle, underlies the comedy film *Passing fancy*. In a simple story of two men who rescue a girl from the streets and then both court her when she is a serving maid, Ozu demonstrates a superb ability to slip easily from the comic scenes in the theatre, at a *naniwa-bushi* (recitation of the heroic stories of the past) where a flea causes havoc in the audience, to the wry humour of the son trying to wake his father by measuring up a blow and then striking his father's shin with a pick handle. Having set this level of somewhat cruel but always controlled humour he can then start a scene as humorous and end it in pathos. The son who has been beaten by his school friends for the stupidity of his father returns home to rain a torrent of blows on his father's head. The father does not react, realizing the justice of the action, but goes over later to his son who, seeing that his father is crying, weeps quietly with him. This wordless encounter born out of comedy suddenly reveals great depths of meaning in a human relationship.

One of the great difficulties for the non-Japanese viewer of Japanese films is the recognition of a set of visual and aural signals that seem to fit the criteria by which we judge our daily experience, but spring from a cultural and social background which differs from our own however similar the surface appears to be. Films couched solidly within the traditional values present a somewhat inscrutable face; those on the ethical left often give the impression of being close to the Occidental spirit but are equally open to misinterpretation.

A brief look at *The Only son* by Ozu will serve to demonstrate that the surface of a Japanese film can act as a mirror to our known reality and thereby hide from our view the depths in which much of the action is really taking place.

The music played behind the opening and closing titles of *The Only son* is instantly recognizable as 'Poor Old Joe' and whilst it is difficult to discover what the exact connotations of such a piece would have been in the Tokyo of 1936 it is obvious from the information of the film that it has no connection with the normal American connotations of the song. The narrative begins with a brief scene set in a village home which acts in terms of the overall structure as a clear piece of exposition. A young school master recommends that Tsune, a widow, put her son, Ryosuke, through secondary education. The school master himself is going to Tokyo in the hope of higher education and opportunity. The fact that further education for her son will require financial sacrifice on her part is only briefly mentioned by the mother. Visual signs here provide, with great economy, information about the status of Tsune. The details of the room put her about the middle of the working class bracket without indicating the economic gulf between the rural workers and their urban equivalents.

Abruptly the story is advanced; Ryosuke has grown up and the mother is to visit her son in Tokyo, for country people the city of dreams and aspirations. There follows a slow revelation of information which, though superbly controlled, is much more direct than Ozu's later style. A series of shots in a taxi reveal Ryosuke, well dressed, showing Tokyo to an admiring mother. Each succeeding sequence takes us nearer the slums and eventually across waste ground to the house, which is on the edge of a very poor area. Once there the son has to reveal his marriage and the fact that he has got a child. Layer by layer the dream has been peeled away to reveal a contradiction of the mother's fond hopes without any overt comment.

The Only son (Ozu, Shochiku 1936)
Mono-no-aware: the acceptance of failed dreams

Ozu, by the time that he made *The Only son*, had begun to refine his technique so that the film presents a cool almost still surface within which the tensions work. The tension in *The Only son* operates on a number of levels all of which have a greater impact if one remembers the strength of the concept of family and duty. There is the natural disappointment of the mother which is balanced by the son's sense of shame that he has not made more of his opportunities, but the contrasts go further to include the difference between the generations; this gap has been widening in Japan as elsewhere in the world except that there it is eroding a stronger set of family bonds and therefore the sense of shock is increased. Contrasts exist too with the intrusion of the modern world into a society that still possesses many of the customs and virtues of the old. Towards the end of the film there is a sequence of shots summing this up. The son leans against the window of his night-school classroom lit by the flashing-neon lights of the city outside. Jazz music floods in from some nearby bar. At home Tsune sits silent and still, dressed in a *kimono* in a small but traditional room. Noises from a nearby restaurant filter through the thin walls. Throughout this the child, Uichi, sleeps unmoving on the floor. The sense of disappointment engendered during this scene is total.

The sudden intervention of tragedy, when the neighbour's boy is kicked by a horse, spurs Ryosuke to give away money to the distraught family, money which he had borrowed to spend on his mother. Life has struck another small but cruel blow against him, not in terms of Aristotelian tragedy – the catastrophe that strikes the powerful – but simply as one of those things that happen; yet this action is the one which restores the son in the eyes of his mother and cancels out most of the sense of failure.

Prior to this Tsune has said in reply to her son's admission of failure in his ambition:

'I don't want you to take the world as it is. It is because I looked forward to your success that I worked. I could work because of you. You are my hope, so get rid of your way of thinking at once. I haven't told you the truth, I have no house in the country, I sold the house and the fields that father left. I am living in a tenement now. But I don't mind what has been done, if only you are resolute enough. I don't want a house and fields. Yours are my hopes, but . . . but you are going to betray my expectation.'

Such a statement would appear in our terms to be emotional blackmail but it is not considered by the Japanese as such. Tsune's speech is only what one would expect a mother to say under such circumstances – she has the right to expect much of her children. It is the conflict between her traditional right and the empirical world that gives this film such poignancy. Ozu does not condemn his characters for their failure, but rather human frailty and fallibility are used as a key to those things in life which lie outside the world of dramatic action and have a sort of beauty in their very existence.

Central to the film and to this attitude to life as expressed by Ozu is a sequence near the middle of the film. Tsune and Ryosuke walk slowly out across waste land. The scene is dominated by the chimneys of the Tokyo incinerator – an image which reappears in a number of Ozu's films and in Gosho's *Where chimneys are seen* (1953). Squatting on their haunches, the chimneys behind the son, the traditional rooftops behind the mother, they talk for the first time about their expectations.

Ryosuke: 'You are disappointed in me, aren't you?' (Long pause) 'I did not intend to be what I am. I sometimes think that I would have been better not to have come to Tokyo. I feel sorry for your trouble that you took to let me come to Tokyo to study.'

Tsune : 'Why do you think of yourself like that? I think your life will get better.'

Ryosuke : 'Of course I am sure it will get better, but sometimes I think that I have come to the end of the game. I wish I had stayed and lived with you in the country.' (They sit in silence for a while. Ryosuke cocks his head and looks up.)

Ryosuke : 'A lark is singing, isn't it?' (Slowly the mother looks up at the sky.)

The implications of the scene on the waste ground are those of the whole film. In terms of the mother's expectations the son is seen as a failure, a failure made more final by the parallel failure of the school-master, now running a neighbourhood restaurant, who had first urged the opportunities offered by Tokyo. The son, a rather poor teacher full of human weaknesses, regards himself as a failure for different reasons. None of these characters can ever win.

The waste ground scene, with its slow pace and unemphatic acting, is typical of Ozu's treatment of human interaction. Though the words themselves are crucial it is the context of the words and the silences between the people which provide the tension. The words alone on the page can do no justice to the film, for they can indicate neither the pace nor the importance of that pace within the context of what has gone before and what is to follow. The final line, like a haiku poem, has no direct reference to what has just been said but in a delicate poetical stroke it encapsulates the two differing worlds of the two generations. It has been said of Ozu that he constructed all his films as though they were silent, then he blended in the words. It is doubtful that the process was ever as simple as that and the words in his films never simply do the job of adding what could not be done by the visuals. They operate at a more refined level by adding extra dimensions of meaning. The scene just described works well without the dialogue, the viewer sensing the feelings of the characters from the setting alone, but the visuals could never have added the poetic reverberations of that last line.

Hope for any change rests with the very young in Ozu's films and it is noticeable that it is usually the grandchildren who make contact with and appear to understand the older generation, bridging the generation in between. This is true of *The Only son* and of *Toda brother and his sisters* (1941), as with most of Ozu's films, and it makes particularly moving the failure of communication between the grandmother and youngest grandson in *Tokyo story*.

Toda brother and his sisters made in 1941 shows little or no influence of a country in an aggressive military mood. At a time when the propaganda machine was stressing the importance of the family as a virtuous unity, within a culture which stresses the strength of the family unit and the duty of children towards their parents, Ozu continued with the blessing of the Ministry of Propaganda to examine the stresses within his model family. Here the death of one of the parents is used to trigger off the story – a recurrent theme in Ozu's films. The stresses placed on the various members of the family as the mother and unmarried daughter move from house to house are used by Ozu to point out the rightness of the traditional values. It is rare that he ever equates the traditional way of life with 'the good' for often his characters can lead a modern life in an external sense and still behave in the best possible moral terms. The widowed daughter-in-law in *Tokyo story* is a good example of this. What may appear to be a straight equation of the older generation with the good arises from the tendency in Ozu's films to point up the clash between brash modern furniture and the quiet of the traditional interior as a parallel to the human contrasts.

In *Toda brother and his sisters* the characters are well delineated so as to fall into recognizable groups; two of the sisters are modern, somewhat acquisitive, strong-willed women, while Shushiro the son is an enigmatic free-moving individual, and Setsuko, the unmarried daughter, a good-willed girl full of the traditional virtues. Place in the middle of these an acquiescent mother and there is the potential for dramatic conflict.

The story of the film is simple enough. A wedding is prepared and the father of the family suddenly has a heart attack and dies. Because of his good nature he has taken the responsibility for the debts of a manufacturing company and now these debts must be paid. This means that the family house and treasure have to be disposed of. The mother, now homeless, moves in succession to the houses of her two daughters and eventually to the family summerhouse by the sea though it is not really fit for habitation. The value judgement that the film contains is heavily weighted towards the conservative traditional virtues of duty, especially those of duty to one's parents.

The richness of the film's texture is pointed out by apparently insignificant gestures so that it is easy for the references and departures from the norm to be missed. The film opens on a long held shot of a courtyard set with two cameras and a row of chairs, all the paraphernalia of a wedding photograph. Little other reference is made to this in the dialogue during the scenes of the photographic session as none is needed for the Japanese audience. After the death of the father which incidentally does not occur on screen, Shushiro Toda, the brother who was absent at the time of the father's death returns to be greeted in the corridor of the house by Setsuko the unmarried daughter. There then follow two incidents which admirably characterize the truly Japanese virtues which are upheld by Ozu. Because she is crying in public Shushiro roughly bundles Setsuko into a side room. This apparent heavy-handedness can be given its true and more reasonable meaning when one considers the difference between public and private behaviour. Not only is the honour of the family protected, but Setsuko is gently prevented from disgracing herself by a public display of emotion. The somewhat stiff behaviour is suddenly broken when Shushiro sticks his hat on Setsuko's head and says 'Don't cry, be of good cheer, forget what's past.' Under the circumstances this is a shocking remark, not so much for its apparent callousness since the Japanese attitude to the dead differs from our own, but more because of its relaxed divergence from the restraint which would have been expected. The second characteristic moment comes when Shushiro confronts his mother to apologize for his absence at the time of his father's death. After he has given his reason, they sit half facing away from each other. The camera does not move. The shot is simply held to create a new statement of the relationship. No words are spoken for there are no words that can be spoken between a mother and a son at such moments.

The artistic device of holding a shot long after it has *seemed* to say all that is necessary – and thereby adding new information – is one used often by Ozu. The effect tends to be one akin to Japanese poetry, for the long-held image devoid of further action demands responses from the audience. A sort of sense reverberation takes place allowing associations on a number of different levels. Tokiko, one of the married sisters, has many of the attributes of modern society, but these form a thin veneer which cracks to reveal her shock on learning that Setsuko is prepared to do manual work to support the mother. Her house, despite its modern furniture, contains a traditional room, which is shown to us after the discussion about work. The shot is still – the room is set for a tea ceremony – and nobody enters, nothing happens. Somehow that shot seems to capture the essence of the conflict between the traditional and the modern. It is a statement made with great economy to describe a complex situation.

Ozu brilliantly outlines, without a word of dialogue, the various emotions in the family during the sequence of the memorial service on the first anniversary of the father's death. Shushiro arrives late and triggers off a set of reactions, each of them hardly noticeable but all of them telling whether the person reacting is glad to see him, or, as in the case of the two married sisters, annoyed that his late arrival has in some way damaged the public image which they so fiercely preserve.

At the end of the film the brother and sister who have stood by the widowed mother are affirmed by Ozu, not as 'good', for they are flawed characters, but as ordinary people with the right sort of approach to life, in whom we can believe. They do not attempt to change anything. They simply try to make the world that they see around them fit to a reasonable sort of human order. As Shushiro says to Setsuko when asking her to agree to an arranged marriage, 'Human desire is infinite, I didn't ask for too much so you mustn't ask for too much either.'

Not asking too much from life appears to be a philosophical attitude that is upheld by many of the characters in Ozu's films. This attitude he places more strongly with his more elderly characters until it seems a sense of resignation. For, seen in the context of the fixed camera positions and non-dramatic lighting that are his distinguishing mark it is easy to regard the actions of the elderly as resigned, but things are rarely as simple as the surface of the film would suggest. To read the actions of the father in *Late spring* (1949) or *Tokyo story* (1953) as resignation would be to debase that quality which Ozu continually, if quietly, praised through the majority of the films he has made: the transcendental quality of acceptance – consciously taking life as it is and knowing that one cannot change it, thus achieving a state of uplifted calm from that knowledge.

Tokyo story (1953) is the distillation of Ozu's attitudes towards the human condition. It is a story full of human, but never romantic, love. For in creating his realistic characters, Ozu rarely invokes romanticism, the staple of all motion picture industries. He himself has avowed that he has no interest in romantic love *per se*, and that his only interest in the various forms of love is in those which are between the members of a family, and he is concerned with romantic love only when it finds an outlet in the form of family love, as between man and wife. Character and incident are superior to action and plot. Ozu has said 'Pictures with obvious plots bore me now. Naturally a film must have some kind of structure or else it isn't a film, but I feel that a picture isn't good if it has too much drama or too much action.' Thus he turns his efforts towards character development and the leisurely disclosure of character.

In *Tokyo story* Ozu examines the relations between three generations. The family becomes the whole world of the film. By creating fully developed characters Ozu demands from the viewer a complete identification and understanding. The internal structure of the film increases this demand, for the time scale is psychological rather than that of a straightforward plot, which would have little meaning in this context. Critic Tsunoe Hazumi's remark 'Ozu's world is one of stillness' is accurate only if one realizes that this stillness, this repose, is the surface beneath which lies the thwarted yet potential violence between people living within the tightly closed circle of a group, especially a family.

The observation of the family group, with the camera at the eye level of a seated onlooker, is apparently so objective, so distant that one is rarely aware

Tokyo Story (Ozu, Shochiku 1953)
Genuine love and understanding between mother and daughter-in-law, a relationship sought for but not found within the family.

of the painter's skill in the creation of the compositions. Ozu, who, like so many other Japanese film directors, first trained as a painter, composed his images with delicate care but in such a way as to avoid any overt 'art'. Actions and words are so deceptively urbane, the parts fit together so organically, that one does not question the reality of the characters and their situation. Had the camera-work been other than it is, such an organic unity would have been broken. The blending of form and content enables Ozu to express what he sees as the core of human life.

It has often been pointed out that Ozu's characters have the rare quality of being 'typical'. Hamlet and Macbeth may demonstrate universality but they cannot in any way be said to be typical, whereas the members of the Hirayama family in *Tokyo story* have the fully rounded characters that go beyond the normal requirements of drama and act in a way which is not only probable but also psychologically correct.

An examination of two scenes from this much discussed film will serve to demonstrate the way in which Ozu uses his skill as a film-maker to support his attitudes towards life.

Subtlety of the pictorial representation, giving rise to reverberations of sense and emotion, is at the heart of the scene in which the grandmother takes the youngest grandchild for a walk. The whole sequence, as so often in Ozu's films, is established and disestablished with the same long-held shot, a technique of repeating in reverse order that sequence of shots which have been used to lead the viewer into a scene. In Ozu's case he often adds a shot of a detail such as a sign or a piece of furniture to the normal sequence of wide shot, medium shot and medium close-up. The resulting pace is gentle and contemplative, the interstices of action being filled with meaningful quiet. In this case against a blank sky, framed by roofs, one traditional one modern, are set the two figures. Information is painted in with the lightest of brushes as the two squat picking grass. Alternately we are provided with the sub-jective view they have of each other. The grandmother is asking the child what he is going to be when he grows up and sees him against a background of a large steel bridge. Out of focus, it echoes the sweep of the traditional architecture yet marks the present industrial development. From the child's point of view the grandmother is presented against a background of industrial chimneys – making her seem sadly out of place, dressed as she is in her *kimono*. These contrasts, so carefully constructed yet so unemphatic, are typical of the additional layers of meaning one finds in these films. Yet Ozu's statement is never critical of one attitude or another; it is sufficient that they exist and have been shown.

At the end of the film when the bereaved grandfather has come to terms with his lonely state, supported only by his youngest daughter who will eventually leave him like the others, the film settles gently into silence – boats in the nearby harbour sound the only notes, the notes of natural activity. Such was the start of the film and it is only at this point that the full circle of the film's structure is complete. In the interim, life has rolled on and

Tokyo Story (Ozu, Shochiku 1953)
Quiet acceptance of the sadness of life – a perfect expression of *mono-no-aware*.

people have acted and reacted, yet it is as if we had returned to the same point in time. Any of the houses in the small town could have offered us a similar story. The difference now is that we have been exposed to Noriko, the widowed daughter-in-law and the one really 'good' person in the whole film; it is she who has helped the old man to come to terms with his future, and one is led to believe that life can be better for Ayoko the youngest as a result of her contact with Noriko.

By his perfect balance of form and content, the control of style and theme, Ozu shows all the foibles of his characters but never demands the total emotional involvement of the audience; he asks us to retain a far wider perspective than his characters are capable of. The characters are the ones who say 'Isn't life disappointing?' Ozu shows all those things that go to make up life, but the act of judgement is left to the audience. Objectivity is not created by any alienating devices such as Godard uses, nor by the clinically judged moment of deflation that one finds in Richard Lester; it is simply by his own apparent detachment, his own assumption that there *is* a wider perspective from which to view these mere mortals, that Ozu communicates a human objectivity and in doing so establishes himself as one of the world's finest film-makers.

8 Mizoguchi: a woman's man

The Vision

Distant mountains
Reflected in its jewel eye
The Dragonfly.

Issa 1762–1826

Whilst Ozu represents that which is most characteristic of Japanese life his films are also furthest from the common denominator of European and American cinema. Experience tells us that the world revealed by film is one in which plot is paramount and movement of character and point of perception are reliable constants. Ozu's films, however, deny that these elements are either necessary or sufficient. Thus the cultural shock is considerable and the viewer is made immediately aware that he is standing on the edge of a culture gap. At the other side stands an artist who does not see his function as one of imposing order on a disordered world.

If one takes Ozu as being on the ethical right wing, a move from the right to the left will reveal several parallel developments. As we move left there is an apparent shift from the group to the individual. At the same time there is an apparent increase in the accessibility of the films; they begin to look more and more as though they might have been made in the West. That plot becomes more important the closer one gets to the ethical left is true, but it is a grave critical mistake to imagine that because these films look Western one can apply the same criteria of content analysis as one would to an American or, say, a French film.

To contrast the stillness of Ozu's films with the overt style of Kurosawa, where lens-technique and cutting are often exploited to create dazzling effects by making the audience aware of the mechanics of the form, is to make the dangerous assumption that because the latter are more immediate in their effect they are therefore more accessible in meaning. Cultural modifiers are constantly at work since, no matter whatever else they may be, these directors are Japanese, and it would be false to make an equation 'Ozu = obscure, Kurosawa = accessible'. This ignores the universality of Ozu's films and the attitudes towards the social structure which permeate Kurosawa's films. Yet such a viewpoint has been fostered by much of the writing about the Japanese cinema, and to a large extent has become the accepted critical norm.

One result of such an attitude has been the view that Mizoguchi can create atmosphere, and a totally credible *milieu* superbly, but little else. Donald Richie has helped to maintain this attitude by quoting the words of a Japanese critic that the locale is the real hero of a Mizoguchi film. In fact

Richie has written of Mizoguchi's *mise-en-scène* to such an extent that an imbalance has been created. He should certainly be acknowledged as one of the world's finest creators of cinematic locale, but to leave it at that is to state only half of the equation. The texture and realistic detail that fill his films serve as a context within which his characters take on a meaningful life. The form informs the content.

Mizoguchi, within the scale that we have created, stands near the centre but still firmly on the ethical right. He films a world whose social system is one immediately recognizable to his Japanese audience. Rarely do any of his characters attempt to act against that system. Most of them suffer under these social codes but their suffering is shown as something that happens, 'that is the way things are', rarely with any implication of 'the way things should be'. The effect that Mizoguchi's films have had on the social system has been great, especially with regard to the position of women within society. But when discussing his films one must be careful to distinguish between the films as they are and the effect that they have had. As the films stand they are solidly within the traditional ethical right, but because of their implicit criticism of the world they should be considered to have elements of the ethical left.

Kenji Mizoguchi was also trained as a painter before becoming a film director. Having worked in Kobe as a newspaper artist for advertisements he began his film career by becoming an actor in the Tokyo studios. A strike by the *onnagata* gave him his chance and he stepped immediately into the position of film director. Some confusion exists about the reason for the strike, pay scales and the incursion of women into films being the most likely causes. Many of the studio technicians went out in sympathy and the producers found themselves without any staff. It is ironic that a man whose entry into films was an almost apologetic gesture on the part of the studios through the loss of their female impersonators should later become possibly the greatest director of films about women that the world has seen. In a career that spanned thirty-four years as a director Mizoguchi made more than ninety feature

Ugetsu Monogatari (Mizoguchi, Daiei 1953)
Sumptuous detail creating a sense of reality which belies the falseness of a ghostly relationship.

Ugetsu Monogatari (Mizoguchi, Daiei 1953)
The meticulously rendered setting of the austere harmony of peasant life.

films. From the very beginning his approach was literary, to the extent that his films tended to be close adaptations of literature, ranging from Kafu Nagai through Shaw and Balzac to Boston Blackie. This eclectic choice is a clue to the change that one can chart through his work.

Once he had settled into the job of directing he set about exploring what is basically the same theme in each of his films; that man is nothing without the love of a woman, that woman's love redeems an often harsh and cruel world. He complements this idea with the theme that woman can only be fulfilled and find her true place in society if she is sustained by the continued love of a man. As a thesis such ideas may be anathema to today's liberation movements – yet they have done much to liberate Japanese women from the position that they held until recently of being second-class citizens.

Outside Japan Mizoguchi is considered a maker of period films but a large part of his output has been on contemporary subjects. As the war approached and controls on the industry were tightened he appears to have moved away from the propaganda machine back into history. In this way he was able to avoid the hand of the political censor but he did not stop commenting on what was relevant to contemporary society. The present is always there in his films. They are not simply beautiful evocations of bygone eras. By a meticu-

59

lous rendering of the texture and minutiae of a period he manages to achieve a convincing impression of the past, yet by careful selection of story and incident he echoes the present time. However, one is never conscious, as with Kurosawa and Kobayashi, of the director saying 'Pay attention, this refers to you and your society'. Since the stylistic control is central to the development of his statements it is worthwhile considering briefly the surface texture of Mizoguchi's films. According to Donald Richie almost any Mizoguchi film can be reduced to a catalogue of beautifully calculated effects which create the atmosphere of his film world, but this is about as valuable as saying that any Van Gogh can be reduced to a definable number of brush strokes and colours. Mizoguchi's films *are* beautiful, staggeringly beautiful, but the beauty of the *mise-en-scène* is there to create total suspension of disbelief and to throw the characters into stark contrast. It can be said that Mizoguchi sometimes heightens reality, such as in the scenes on the lake and the famous picnic scene from *Ugetsu monogatari* (1953), or in the poetic use of sound in *Sansho dayu* (1954), but these effects are so woven into the overall texture of the film that they rarely strike an obtrusive note.

Sansho dayu (Mizoguchi, Daiei 1954)
The interdependence of brother and sister thrown into sharp contrast against a background of peasant slavery.

Mizoguchi's films are characterized by a remarkable freedom of camera movement. It is true that he liked to use the long-held shot to create atmosphere, often taken from a distance, observing the characters across an intervening space – but the overriding device is camera movement. That critics tend not to mention this is a mark of the great skill with which he prevents it from being obtrusive. In many of his films the camera tracks and cranes with a fluidity rarely seen in the cinema. Yet none of it is virtuoso work; the camera moves only when necessary. This ability to move his camera with confidence allows him to construct long scenes in which by constantly changing the dynamics of the frame he can shift the audience's point of focus to just that character or object that he requires at that moment of the plot. At the same time he uses very few cuts. Much of this visual quality must have been contributed by Kazuo Miyagawa, the director of photography on a number of his films since the Second World War.

The formal structure of the films is certainly Mizoguchi's and here one can see the influence of his art training. Like Kurosawa and Ichikawa, Mizoguchi was trained in a school of Western-style art – at that time a severely formalized approach. It is not artistic narcissism which makes him start and finish *Ugetsu monogatari* with what are effectively mirror versions of the same shot, a crane down from a wide shot of the village at the beginning and a crane up from a grave to show the village once more, thus neatly drawing in the circle. This is a visual cliché, but the Japanese are a people who delight in the cliché, whether literary or visual.

Formal structures of composition often lead a director into the use of visual motif, sometimes even superseding theme by this, as in the case of some of the films of Ford and Hawks. Mizoguchi, while he lets the theme remain constant, continually changes the context, thus maintaining the predominance of the theme. That is not to say that there are not certain visual motifs which figure in his films; flowing water often acts in this way but is far from being a personal signature since flowing water as an image of the passage of time and life is one of the central figures of Japanese poetry, literature and art. Life will continue whatever mere humans do.

Oharu, in *The Life of Oharu* (1952), has little or no choice in what she does. Society has created a set of rules and regulations which predetermine her downward path and what society sees as her human weaknesses only serve to quicken her fall from grace. Questions of morality are not raised – audiences are not expected to make judgements in the way that we have come to expect as a result of our literary conditioning. Nor does the director make a value judgement on his characters. He simply states that this is the way things are. Rarely do any of his characters actively fight to change the social structure. At one point in the story Oharu has been discovered in a clandestine relationship with Katsusuke. Later, when separated, they both express a case they know to be hopeless; she to the nuns she has been forced to join, he to those who are about to execute him. Oharu and Katsusuke both plead for a time when there will be no class distinctions and people can follow their own reasons and the dictates of their own hearts, and this cross-cut sequence is about the nearest that Mizoguchi comes to making an overt criticism through the mouths of his characters. Even so this is an impossible wish rather than an active protest.

The critical thrust is achieved by creating a meticulous image of a period and its social structure. Once this has been done then Mizoguchi can use his camera to indicate subtly the social pressures, and it is here that his ability to create superb images begins to have a meaningful power.

The freely moving camera is often used to give the audience a complete

view of a scene, focusing attention on what are to the Japanese significant details; once this has been achieved the character or plot elements are allowed to play off against these elements. The opening scenes of *The Story of the last chrysanthemums* (1939) contain some quite extraordinary camera movements as we are smoothly transported from the stage of the Kabuki theatre through the veritable warren of rooms behind the stage picking up parts of conversations and actions in a way which makes even the weavings of the camera and the sound control in Altman's *M*A*S*H* look heavy-handed. By establishing this credible world narrative impact is gained by the introduction of a woman, Otoku, into an exclusively male environment. The stillness of some of the long-held compositions looking through one room to another in which the action is taking place is in direct opposition to the ideological conflict as a woman becomes active in furthering the career of her chosen man. Such alternation of flow and stillness allows for the poignancy of the film's final sequence which is cross-cut between the actor in a boat parade receiving the accolade of the crowd and Otoku dying in a room overlooking the river. Editing brings these two actions together in such a way that the audience realizes the impossibility of Otoku being saved.

In a similar way camera movement delineates the context of the action in the opening sequence of *The Lady of Musashino* (1951), for after the shot which sets the image for the rest of the film – water flowing over reeds – a single, long, looping crane shot introduces the characters and the neighbouring houses that are the conflicting elements of the story. With consummate ease the camera leads us in to the son and daughter digging in the garden just as they unearth a skull. The mark of death hangs over these characters from the first encounter.

When taken out of context some of these camera moves may have the air of a *coup de théâtre* about them but blended into the fabric of the film they become simply the correct, apposite, artistic gesture. When Oharu and her parents are forced to leave their home town, a sequence of moving camera shots leads smoothly into a startling effect. As the family cross a bridge and walk away from the camera, the view-point slides under the bridge to block out the top part of the screen leaving the characters trudging across a narrow wedge of skyline. The effect though harsh is not simple virtuosity – one is more aware of the effect emotionally than photographically. Its power comes from the parallel between the crushing of three people by social regulations and the visual crushing of the small figures by the enormous black masses on the screen. At that precise point of the narrative the single image has the value of a thousand words.

The ability to create realistic period films is a rare enough skill and there are only a handful who have ever created period films which are accurate in detail yet make no condescension to contemporary society in the behaviour of the characters. Bergman achieved outstanding success with *Virgin spring* and *The Seventh seal*, Jancso revivifies more recent history with a somewhat surreal touch in *The Round-up* and to a certain extent Schaffner in *The War lord* evokes a credible and self-sufficient world.

New tales of the Taira clan (*Shin heike monogatari*, 1956), a much neglected film, surely establishes Mizoguchi as Japan's finest director of the period film with its scale of grandeur and superb narrative control but, in fact, his concentration on the period film developed slowly. It was really with the coming of the wartime controls that Mizoguchi departed from contemporary subjects.

opposite: *The Life of Oharu* (Mizoguchi, Shin Toho 1952)
The poignancy of the still image in the flowing narrative of a courtesan's slow destruction by a social system.

Like many others he sought his material in the literature of classical Japan (he even made two versions of the story of the forty-seven Ronin) preferring Chikamatsu and Saikaku (*The Life of Oharu*) to modern writers such as Mishima or Abe. His was a world in which the system rather than the individual was at fault. Kinoshita states that women are to blame for their own troubles and Naruse paints an even bleaker picture – none have managed the quiet elegance, the *shibui* of Mizoguchi's films, and few have managed to see the past without nostalgia. When Mizoguchi died, Kurosawa, a man whose films sometimes verge on the *hade*, the loud and vulgar opposite of *shibui*, said: 'Now that Mizoguchi has gone, there are very few directors left who can see the past clearly and realistically.'

Now that Mizoguchi has gone there are few directors left who can see human beings, especially women, as clearly and as realistically.

9 Wives and mothers

An Enquiry to a Person in Etchigo Province

Snow at which
Two people looked – this year
Has it also fallen?

Matsuo Basho 1644–1694

Outside the Japanese cinema there have been few who have made successful films about women, as opposed to films for women. This is not to suggest that the Japanese film industry has studiously avoided sentimentality and *grand guignol* in its films about women, far from it, but it is important to note that they have produced a substantially greater body of work about women than any other national cinema. Like the Indian cinema many films are made which are little more than romantic fantasies. Like the American cinema many films are made which are idealized love stories. Bette Davis in a crinoline acting the untamed passionate creature finds a parallel in many films of the fifties. When *Gone with the wind* was re-released in Japan in the early sixties it ran for months to packed houses of largely female audiences. The major difference between the love story film made outside Japan and the home product is that there is a tendency for the Japanese love affair to be a thwarted one, a relationship doomed from its inception and most likely ending in suicide. To the Japanese there is a beauty and poignancy in the obvious impossibility and impermanence of the love affair which is reflected in literature, theatre and the cinema.

Across the full spectrum of genres and types of films within the Japanese cinema can be found films with women as their subjects, from Ozu's delicate family portrayals and Mizoguchi's deep understanding of both the courtesan of the past (*The Life of Oharu*) and her modern equivalent (*Women of the night*, 1948) to the sexploitation and girl-gangster films of the modern cinema. With notable exceptions this aspect of cinema has seen remarkably little attack on whatever the social and political norms were at the time. In a male-dominated industry such as that of the Japanese there has to date been no opportunity for the emergence of an oriental Agnes Varda or Lisa Wertmuller, and we are unlikely to see a Japanese *Wanda*. Despite the growing emancipation of the Japanese woman, the overall effect of the social system and the firmly rooted attitudes of the majority serve to precondition the products of the film industry so that they maintain the social status quo and reinforce traditional behaviour. When an industry which is in the main conservative does manage to make a film about women which satirizes or criticizes male attitudes then this is an occasion of importance. When these

Women of the night (Mizoguchi, Mizoguchi Productions 1948)
Mizoguchi's sympathetic but unsentimental treatment of the postwar prostitute.

are seen against the total production figures they remain a small, though significant, percentage.

Criticism of the predominant attitudes towards women are implicit in the films of Mizoguchi. The converse is found in Naruse with his constant hinting that the problems of woman are largely their own fault, though he modifies this in *Floating clouds* (1955) to include the influence of the past as one of the factors conditioning women's place in society. More firm in his belief that woman had only woman to blame for her hard lot was Keisuke Kinoshita. In *Carmen's pure love* (1952) he created a heroine who, being a 'modern' girl, took upon herself the decisions to act when necessary. Having embarked upon this course she sails straight into the face of society and all its idiocies and anomalies. From this confrontation Kinoshita creates a satirical picture of modern Japan, but at the same time affords little sympathy for his central character. The following year in *Clouds at twilight* he was able to portray this clash with a conservative and uncompromising social structure in a more gentle and understanding portrayal. Yet he had moved far away from the traditional view that the inequalities of women's position within Japanese society were inevitable – the view which permeates Ozu's films – or that it was sad and to be regretted, as seen in Jukichi Uno's *Extreme sadness* (1956).

Whilst films such as these were made they were not really representative of the major 'tendencies' in films about women. With the introduction of the *Shomin-geki* and its concentration on middle-class realism there was a natural concern for the domestic setting for these dramas. Central to the Japanese home is the role that the mother plays within the family structure – that of a strong anchor for the family unit, who though deferential towards the male head of the family maintains the position of power within the home. At the same time she has been placed in a subservient position by social tradition (though this has been steadily lessening since the turn of the century, and especially since the last war). Such an apparent dichotomy of roles has produced a tension within the whole social structure of Japan, usually met with a sense of resignation. In the genre of films known as *haha-mono* or 'mother films' this sense of resignation is often allied to an overpowering sense of obligation. Having achieved the status of Mother, a status more desirable to the Japanese than the status of wife (which if we are to believe the evidence of the Hollywood films was the ultimate goal for any American woman), the genre then imposes great burdens upon her. These were usually in the form of widowhood, errant children, a desperate need for money often leading to prostitution; the final obligation that could be thrust upon the mother was the arrival of either her parents or those of her husband. All these impositions had to be borne by her and it was part of the genre that she remained firm and unbending in her attitudes, winning through to the end to the rapturous tears of the audience. The behaviour of these mothers must seem stubborn and often irrational to the non-Japanese viewer but it must be remembered that they are performing within a rigidly defined set of parameters, part of a unit rather than individuals, which served to reinforce traditional attitudes towards the family in the minds of the audience.

Such was the belief in the justice of this view of the family that for a considerable period before and during the war a studio like Shochiku under the direction of Shiro Kido stressed the need for a sound family life in all its films.

The *haha-mono* reached its peak just before the last war and was upheld through the war by the Ministry of Propaganda. Once the new peace had arrived and the social structure had begun to modify itself under the influence of America, the *haha-mono* went into rapid decline and was replaced by the *tsuma-mono* or 'wife film'. The films of this genre are usually concerned with her personal problems, especially those of her identity as an individual. As such they give opportunity for expression by ethical left film-makers more than had previously been the case. Unfortunately this opportunity was rarely taken. Even after the war the examination of the individual was not a majority concern.

Just as the *haha-mono* resolved itself into a set of clichés, so too did the *tsuma-mono*. The wife seeking a sense of identity in an often empty marriage enters into a passing and trivial love affair and through this rediscovers her love for her husband. Rarely do these films delve deep into character. With characteristic uninterest in narrative complexity many of these films degenerated into simple sob-stories – but were none the less popular for that.

Within the criteria applied to literature or drama the Japanese do not have a strict equivalent of the term 'tragedy' – the term *higeki* translates better as

Trumpet boy (Sekigawa, Toei 1955)
A thoroughly melodramatic blend of bathos and sentimentality.

'sad play' and with the exception of great artists such as Ozu, Kinoshita and Naruse most of the film-makers engaged in this field have taken the stuff of life which could give birth to genuine tragedy and made of it sad little melodramas. So unashamedly tear-jerking are many of these films that they are rated one-, two- or three-handkerchief films.

In the terms of the thesis that has been set out in this book the vast majority of the films about women are solidly on the ethical right with a tendency in the *tsuma-mono* to move towards a more central position. There are few opportunities for the women to make a free choice rather than act within a rigidly defined set of standards. The romantic fantasies, whether period or contemporary, make little comment on the state of women but rather serve the need for escapism. The popular series of 'three girl' films move only within the bounds of standard social behaviour. In these films three girls, representing the traditional, the modern and the 'liberated' woman go through a series of happy and often musical adventures, often set within a college situation, yet in the end they make the totally predictable and socially acceptable decisions. They are given little chance to make free choices and by acting eventually in the 'right' way, despite the apparent dangers of their modern behaviour, they re-establish the virtue of conformity and satisfy the hopes of the middle-class audience.

In the late fifties there emerged a new type of film featuring women. These were the 'nudies'. Films like Manao Horiguchi's *Underwater romance* (1957) and Kosho Nomura's *The Woman by the lonely sea* (1958) showed nudity on the screen for the first time – and this was only ten years since the first Japanese screen kiss had been seen. The first of the nude films had stories but they were banal and simply used female groups like the girl pearl divers to satisfy producers' opportunism. This was to be the beginning of the move towards the sexploitation or 'pink' films that have grown to take up nearly half of the cinema's production by 1973.

Even within the modern 'tendencies' of the Japanese cinema, films about women seem to uphold the view that women must conform to all the principles of group identity and even subjugation to the male. The modern trend of gangster or *yakuza* films, which were enormously popular at the end of the sixties, was to have gangs composed of sexily-dressed, sensual girls. The first impression is one of a complete break with all the traditional attitudes but a closer look will show that the gangs are simply a modern version of the long-held view of the strength of the group identity and loyalty.

There are, however, certain films within these groupings which do take a more considered look at the Japanese woman, treating her as an individual capable of making her own decisions. In addition to those already cited Susumu Hani must be noted for a number of films.

Having begun his career making documentary films Hani made his first feature film in 1961. His second film *A Full life* (1962) told the story of an actress moving from one lover to the next in an attempt to find out something about herself. Ambivalent in its message it brought a new freshness to the screen for Hani used all his documentary techniques, filming in the streets and using amateur actors. This gave his films a recognizable quality of contemporary reality which was to serve him in all his films, especially *She and he* (1963). Sachiko Hidari (in real life Hani's wife), plays a middle-class housewife living comfortably in a suburban flat. When some shacks on nearby waste land burn down she meets a rag picker who lives with a blind girl and a dog. A friendship develops between Naoko, the housewife, and the rag picker. She has a natural concern for these unfortunate people and her sense of guilt is increased when she learns that the rag picker had been at university with her husband. She forces her husband to offer the man a job which he declines. Then when the little girl falls ill Naoko takes her into the flat, much to the annoyance of her husband who sends the girl to a hospital. By the time workers move in to knock down the rest of the shacks, the rag picker has been separated from the girl whom he had come to regard as his child and eventually his dog dies. Naoko has achieved nothing with her involvement in someone else's life, but she has of her own free will made a gesture. It is this gesture, albeit fruitless, which helps her to come to terms with herself and at the same time gain some understanding of her husband.

In Naoko, Hani has managed to create a credible Japanese woman who by her concerns becomes a universal symbol for the majority of Japanese women. The *milieu* of her life is explored in detail by a free-flowing camera matched by subtle and unobtrusive acting. The context is traditionally middle-class and the final actions of all of the characters are close to *mono-no-aware*. The essential difference here is that Naoko has acted as a free individual and has attempted to cut across the traditional responses and change a situation. That she achieved little is not important for her gesture takes this film out of its apparent right-wing stance – it suggests to the viewer that there is a value in individual identity.

In one sense, by making such a sensitive portrayal of the Japanese housewife Hani had exposed the problem of being Japanese in a modern world. Hani looked again at the problem of being Japanese – from a male point of view in *Bwana toshi* (1965) and the female point of view again in *Bride of the Andes* (1966). In both cases he removes his characters from their homeland and forces them to consider in a new light all those things which had been the precepts of their life in Japan. Hidari stars in *Bride of the Andes* as a postal bride for an anthropologist living with the Incas in the Andes. Separated from all that she knows, faced with a new culture and a new husband she is forced to reconsider all her responses and attitudes – she has to learn to adapt and at the same time learn what makes her peculiarly Japanese. Whilst this film can be read as an unusual love story, for she does grow to love her husband and stays on to continue his work after he has been killed in the collapse of a trench, it has a more important place in the Japanese cinema than might at first appear since it shows a pattern of self-examination unusual to a character such as the one played by Hidari. It is a strong move towards the ethical left contained within an apparently middle-class, though exotic, love story.

She and he (Hani, Iwanami 1963)
In her middle-class context Naoko struggles ineffectively for independence of thought and action.

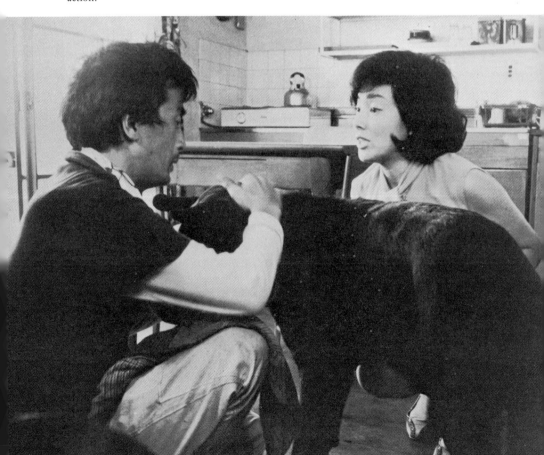

Bride of the Andes (Hani, Iwanami 1966)
An examination of the essential quality of being Japanese by removal from the Japanese context.

   The removal of a character from the normal social context in order to make that character perform a process of ratiocination is an extreme method, and, as will be seen in the next chapter, is not a necessary adjunct to a film which might be placed on the ethical left. It is however a device employed by Hiroshi Teshigahara in *Woman of the dunes* (1964) which whilst not strictly a film about a woman is worth considering in this context.
   Teshigahara, yet another of the Japanese film directors who was first trained as a painter, was enabled to set up his own film production company with the help of his father's money. After making a number of documentary films he formed an association with the novelist Kobo Abe, who has remained his sole scenarist. Together they have pushed further into the surreal – a major preoccupation of Teshigahara when he was a painter. *Woman of the dunes*, Teshigahara's first international success, is filled with a meticulous rendering of surface reality in what is a surreal situation. A wandering entomologist accepts hospitality for a night in a house at the bottom of a sand pit and the next morning finds that he cannot escape. Like the insects that he has been examining, he too becomes a specimen, studied both by the villagers and the camera.

Woman of the dunes (Teshigahara, Toho/Teshigahara 1964)
A single task becomes the raison d'être for the maintenance of independent existence.

Woman of the dunes (Teshigahara, Toho/Teshigahara 1964)
An almost surrealistic presentation of the textures of skin and flowing sand.

Examination of the self as one looks at insects under a microscope has been a recurrent theme in recent Japanese films and literature. In this case the situation is complicated in human terms since the house is inhabited by a woman who toils like a dung beetle to hold back the shifting sands which threaten to engulf the village. Here the woman in a role which is subservient to the rest of the village has been given an enormous burden of obligation which, until the arrival of the man, she had accepted without question. The developing relationship between the man and the woman, as he slowly grows to understand her position and join her in the task, is shown to us by some of the most seductive camera work yet seen. Flowing sand becomes liquid and indistinguishable from human skin in scenes which carry a far greater erotic charge than any overtly erotic film. The man eventually makes love to the woman in front of the villagers, for two reasons: he desires her and he can thereby pay the price of escape, since the villagers consider her too ugly for anyone to love. Once he has escaped, however, the man returns voluntarily to the hole to test his theory of water collection from the sand.

This surrealist activity somewhat masks the real theme of two people, each of whom were in their own way stolidly conservative, forced into self-examination through confrontation with another human being and at the same time cut off from any social context which might have provided a soothing set of responses. The opportunity is provided for individual re-action and thought – a mode far removed from the ethical right.

Woman in Japanese cinema can therefore be seen as the presenter of a set of attitudes and responses which are in the main traditional and conservative less often in a liberal central path and rarely of the ethical left.

10 Kurosawa and Ichikawa: feudalist and individualist

In the Paddy Field

Women planting rice:
Only their song
Free from the mud.

Raizan 1653–1716

A few days before the Christmas of 1971, a housemaid found Akira Kurosawa slumped in a half-filled bath. His neck, elbows, wrists, and hands had been slashed in twenty-one places. He had apparently attempted suicide. Hospital spokesmen said that his recovery would take two weeks.

Of all the Japanese film directors Akira Kurosawa is probably better known to audiences outside Japan than any other. Certainly his work is better documented than any of his compatriots. His films have the appearance of being so close to the cinema of the West that they are easily assimilated by an audience that reads them with the same critical criteria as they apply to their own films. It was not surprising to find that a film such as *The Seven samurai*, almost an archetypal 'western', should be remade as *The Magnificent seven* (Kurosawa's film was first released in the USA under that title) or that 'The man with no name' blasting his tight-lipped way through *A Fistful of dollars* should have been modelled on *Yojimbo*. To a non-Japanese audience Kurosawa's films do not seem 'Japanese' in the way that the films of Ozu or Mizoguchi do, yet Kurosawa has maintained that all his inspiration and observation has been from that which is essentially Japanese. Is there any paradox in this? Is our concept of what is 'Japanese' in need of revision?

For many years it has been maintained, especially by Donald Richie, that Kurosawa is the great humanist of the Japanese film, the man of the true ethical left. The dying Watanabe in *Ikiru* (*Living*, 1952) represents Man as an individual working out the rationale for his own actions, working against a system whose very existence is essential within the scheme of the film. Nakajima in *Record of a living being* (1955) embodies the ethical left humanism that Richie claims, though he is driven out of the normal behaviour-patterns by his fear, as do the central characters in *The Idiot* (1951) and *Lower depths* (1957). But what of the central characters in *Sanshiro sugata* (1943) *Rashomon* (1950) *The Seven samurai* (1954) *Throne of blood* (1957) *The Hidden fortress* (1958) *Yojimbo* (1961) and even *Red beard* (1965)? How do these films fit into the scheme of the ethical left, which was after all first developed by Donald Richie?

There has been a critical tendency, fostered by the available writing, to

Ikiru (Kurosawa, Toho 1952)
The master becomes the pupil as the dying Watanabe follows his cloaked guide through the demi-monde.

regard everything that has been made by Kurosawa as being humanist and moreover to regard them blindly as humanist in terms of Occidental society and its values.

The major part of his work has put forward an intensely 'humanist' view of the world, but it is humanism of a Japanese origin, stimulated by Japanese society and voiced to the world by a film-maker who looks to his own samurai ancestry and the classical arts of Japan for his cultural roots.

Many of the misconceptions about the films have arisen from a critical attention to the central character, which notes certain behavioural patterns, but ignores the context within which these actions occur. In a Kurosawa film the social context is of crucial importance to the relevance of each of the characters' actions, and is a large part of any comment being made by the film, as in many Japanese films the director assumes that the audience is fully conversant with a particular social or historical context. This assumption is of course made by the film-maker in every country yet we do not often consider the relevance of our films in a context which differs considerably from our own.

Occasionally the films themselves provide enough background information about the various social groups and their codes for the non-Japanese viewer to cope reasonably with the action of the characters within a film. Such is the case with *The Seven samurai* and is a contributory factor in its overseas success. But it is not the case in many other films. *Ikiru* only has its full impact when one understands the enormity of the action of Watanabe as he fights against the indifference of the bureaucratic structures. A clerk in his position, even as head of a section, is never expected to challenge the very system that his long years of conformity have supported and strengthened.

Since Kurosawa's films themselves have been extensively documented, it is not the purpose of this work to detail each of them chronologically. In order to place his films within the scheme of this survey and to clarify his particular type of humanism, it will be useful to look briefly at Kurosawa himself, the formal structure of his films and at the recurrent themes within them.

Kurosawa has often been granted samurai ancestry and there is much in his work which is evocative of Zen and *bushido*, but his parents were far from rich and his father was a teacher with an enthusiasm for physical education. After leaving school, at which he was class president, Kurosawa entered the Doshusha School of Western Painting. In 1936, realizing that he would not be able to make a living out of painting, he succeeded in being selected as an assistant director with the P.C.L. Studios. Thus at the age of twenty-six he began his career in films. Under the apprenticeship scheme still current in the industry he was assigned to Kajiro Yamamoto and a fruitful teacher-pupil relationship grew up. How much this affected Kurosawa is difficult to assess but it is noticeable that many of his films centre on just such a relationship.

The experience of working with Yamamoto combined with his training as a painter in the Western style gave to Kurosawa an unerring ability to create realistic *milieux* for his films. This is never simply a meticulous recreation of environment, whether contemporary or period – although they were certainly that – but also making the setting, the quality of the light and even the weather conditions essential and integral to the content of the film. The blend of surface texture and internal sense and mood is as perfect as has been achieved in the cinema.

The Seven samurai (Kurosawa, Toho 1954)
Kurosawa's repeated use of a circular pattern reinforces the sense of unity amongst the peasant warriors.

Kurosawa's method of creating a film is also important to the quality of the final artifact. As has already been mentioned the initial step is a literary one, allowing the characters and the plot to develop each other, yet the finished result never looks like the visual illustration of a literary record. Though he may not create his story-board until the script has been completed he does this with the greatest of care, working out all the details of every image before a single frame of film is exposed. So demanding is he of the quality of his images that he developed, starting with *The Seven samurai*, a multi-camera technique, in order to get the most sustained performance possible, yet knowing all the time exactly which sections of film in which cameras would appear in the final version. Kurosawa said at a press conference in Avignon in 1971:

'I work with several cameras, a technique which I experimented with for the first time for the battle-sequence in *The Seven samurai*. This has allowed me to have both continuity and to integrate into the film the precise moment when one actor feels himself to be inside the skin of the character. Equally it is for the same reason that I use the long lens a lot, for the distance permits the actor to forget the camera more easily. . . . In general I use lenses of 100, 200 and 500 mm. with a very small aperture.'

Such a method demands extreme control by the director and as a result he has either supervised the editing or done it himself – even taking all the film into a locked room and having food sent in until the job was complete, if we are to believe some of the stories that he has perpetuated. It is not for nothing that he gained the name of *Tenno* or Emperor (although, as Donald Richie points out, this name is used by others in the industry, not by those who have worked with him). He is renowned for the care which he takes with his films and has the doubtful distinction of having taken the longest time in the history of Japanese cinema to make two of his films. *The Seven samurai* and *Red beard* took eighteen months and two years respectively.

A still from an Ozu film is instantly recognizable as an Ozu image. This is not true of the individual images from a Kurosawa movie (with the exception of those images which have become recognizable by virtue of the number of times they have been printed). The style of his films lies not in the single image or the archetypal composition but in the way that all the images are blended together into a stunning rhythmic flow that has much in common with musical form. The cutting rhythms of his films appear to be faster than those of other contemporary directors, a feeling which is increased by his use of exciting and tense screen dynamics, contrasting with the placid, gentle images of Ozu. His work is also characterized by a brilliant use of textures, harsh almost tactile surfaces which bring a new realism to monochrome movies. In *The Seven samurai* the first use of the recently developed long lens lifted audiences bodily into the middle of a rain-soaked battle to experience the confused impressions of those in the fight. The power of such effects derives from the fact that they were always organically developed from the content of the film, and never exploited simply for the chance of a *coup de théâtre*.

Kurosawa has said that when he photographs something it is merely to get material for the editing process. From such a comment, which should be treated with the same amount of reserve applicable to all comments by film-makers about their own work, one must not think that Kurosawa does not take trouble over the images. A brief consideration of almost any section of any one of his films would serve to demonstrate that there is an almost perfect blend of light, frame-dynamics, movement, perspective and composition to create an organic whole. *Rashomon* glistened with a strangely luminescent quality, light bursting from foliage and sword blades or gleaming from flesh and clothing.

The photographic style of Kurosawa's films has given each film an exciting sense of dynamism. The still beauty of parts of *Rashomon* is counter-pointed by supple camera movement varying from the fluid stalking round the trees during each of the versions of the fight to the brilliant loping descent of the running Mifune through the trees, a movement totally expressive of animalistic energy. This startling effect, achieved by moving the camera along a short curving track and panning with the figure running on a wider concentric arc, is again used on the galloping horsemen in the rain-soaked forest of *Throne of Blood*. Here too the use of stark contrasts is notable. The Noh theatre influenced the stylised composition of the throne-room as Washizu, the Macbeth of this superb adaptation, talks to his wife. Without moving, she dominates every composition as she does his mind. What Kurosawa has added over and above the Noh influence is the figure riding restlessly round and round the courtyard in the background, representative of Washizu's mental turmoil. The arrival of messengers motivates the use of one of Kurosawa's best-known stylistic devices – that of cutting from a relatively static scene to one full of action, shot on a long lens with the main line of action along the axis of the lens, often with figures or horsemen thundering powerfully towards the viewer. The same is seen in all of his period films: the squat figure of Takashi Shimura, the leader of the samurai, running with sword drawn into the middle of the village in *The Seven samurai*, the advancing clans in *Yojimbo*, or the sudden cut in *Sanjuro* from the interior of

Sanjuro (Kurosawa, Toho/Kurosawa Films 1962)
The maintenance of a feudal order as samurai look to Tsubaki Sanjuro as their natural leader.

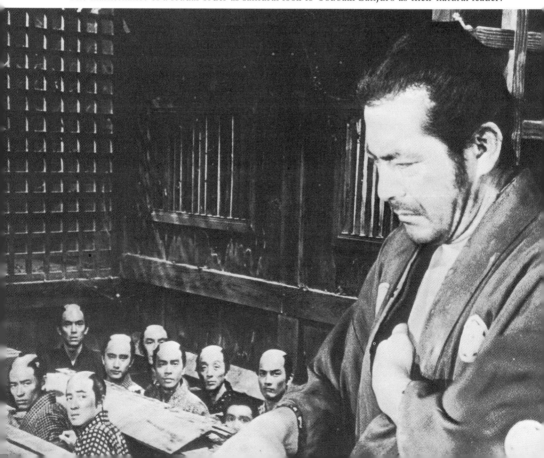

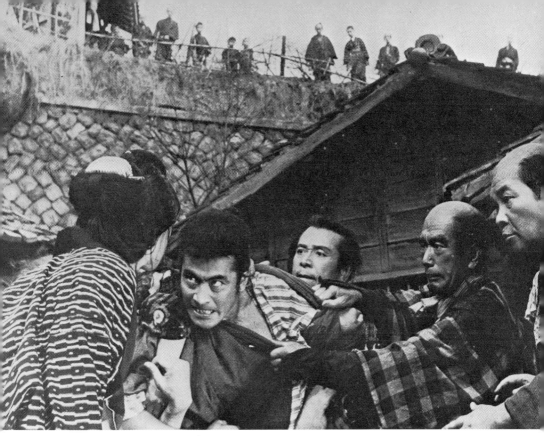

Lower depths (Kurosawa, Toho 1957)
A social microcosm overlooked by a dispassionate world.

the house with Mifune in close-up to the view along the street outside as Tatsuya Nakadai leads the enemy forces in on horseback, all of them bunched together by the telephoto lens into a mass of armoured bodies. This style of shooting, keeping action in the line of the lens, can be seen in the work of cameramen from other cultural backgrounds. Perhaps because it demands open spaces this style is less suited to contemporary subjects although films such as *Point blank* and *Bullitt* have used it to great advantage. The veteran cameraman Lucien Ballard has of late been employing a photographic style not unlike that of the Japanese, most noticeably in *The Wild bunch* and *Junior Bonner*.

Compression of elements by the use of the long lens is also evident, though less obvious, in the contemporary films. *High and low* employs this crushing effect to pull together a house in the poor part of town and a villa on the high ground so that one is dominated by the other. However, there is in these films the tendency to allow the camera to probe and prowl through the crowded jungle of the modern world – as in the nervous snooping of the camera as it follows Watanabe into the *demi-monde* of artificial nightlife in *Ikiru*. The effect of probing into a private and protected world is enhanced by the use of the multi-camera technique which, whilst giving continuity to action, also imbues a scene with a sense of being closed in from all sides. Paradoxically, the result is not usually claustrophobic since our own eyes have replaced the walls surrounding the action and the human interaction is revealed to us. The one film in which this technique is used to generate claustrophobia is *Lower depths* in which, paradoxically, the cameras point outwards to show that the walls of the hollow, in which a social microcosm exists, are overlooked by a dispassionate world.

Kurosawa is a master of construction in that he can develop a sequence in such a way that the culminating image, whilst organic to the circumstances of the action, becomes a symbolic statement. One thinks of the steel wall sliding irrevocably between the rich industrialist and the poor kidnapper in *High and low*; the long-held shot in *The Seven samurai* on the sprawled body of Mifune lying dead on a footbridge as the rain washes the mud of battle from his exposed buttocks, or the final mist-shrouded courtyard scene in *Throne of blood* in which the evil figure of Washizu, having advanced like a gross toad through a hail of arrows, kneels like a bedraggled porcupine before the expressionless troops. Each film contains moments such as these, akin in quality to the best of Japanese *haiku* in which the particular is made universal. Tricks of the camera are rarely employed by Kurosawa to achieve any of these effects, and when such tricks are used they are used sparingly and only when apposite. Slow motion is twice selected for a dying fall in *The Seven samurai*, and speeded motion, though hardly noticeable, throws Washizu down the final flight of steps. Imitators and devotees of Kurosawa have been less restrained and slow motion deaths now abound in Westerns, both American and Italian. In the work of a director such as Sam Peckinpah there are so many visible influences of Kurosawa that one questions Peckinpah's claim that he has never seen a Kurosawa film. The slaughter in the opening sequence of *The Wild bunch* bears great similarity to the battles of *The Seven samurai* – a feeling strengthened by the shot immediately after the battle as L.Q. Jones and Strother Martin run towards the camera amongst the bodies in the street just as if they had sprung from the period world of Kurosawa.

Throne of blood (Kurosawa, Toho 1957)
The death of Washizu in the most magnificent adaptation of Shakespeare to the screen.

The Idiot (Kurosawa, Toho 1951)
One of the most notable and stylish of the many adaptations of Russian literature to be found in Japanese cinema.

With the notable exception of *They who step on a tiger's tail* which is based on the theatrical style of the Noh, Kurosawa's films have created the impression of realism, firstly through the surface texture which gives to the viewer a sense of a genuine physical context, and secondly with the way in which he allows his characters to interact with that environment. This interaction of character and environment is an important feature of his films since it enables us to classify them.

The most obvious classification is the period film, the *Jidai-geki*: *Rashomon*, *The Seven samurai*, *The Hidden fortress*, *Throne of blood*, *Yojimbo*, *Sanjuro* and *Red beard*. In these the careful reconstruction of the period setting is matched by a very precise manner of playing. The actors in these films manage, under Kurosawa's direction, to create much more than a breathtaking skill with the sword. Rather they create a whole social order from peasant to lord which is credible in all its aspects. The warriors are men of genuine samurai skill, men for whom the real fight takes place during the confrontation, before the swords are drawn from their scabbards, rather than exponents of the noisy swordslashing thud–and–blunder that one can see in the work of lesser artists.

There is also that class of films by Kurosawa which derive their inspiration from Russian literature, notably *The Idiot* and *Lower depths*, and those which owe much to contemporary fiction, especially the thriller: *Drunken angel*, *Stray dog*, *The Bad sleep well* and *High and low*. Through these films Kurosawa chose to confront the troubled society that was Japan after the war. However, it was in *Ikiru* (the fight against official obtuseness by a man aware that he was dying of cancer), *Record of a living being* (an intelligent man driven out of his social confines by the fear of atomic warfare), and *The Silent duel* (a doctor faced with the dilemma of syphillis), that Kurosawa opened an all-out attack on those social attitudes which he felt were negative and held back social growth.

There is one element in all of Kurosawa's films which is of prime importance and which has been ignored by many of his critics. The characters in Kurosawa's films interact with their environment; they are realistic in that they condition and are conditioned by the social context in which they live. Now while Richie has made this point, he has chosen to ignore the nature of that social structure. For this society is seen by a Japanese and since it derives from Japanese culture it is not surprising to find that the structure is feudal, not only in the period films since they reconstruct an overtly feudal society, but also in the films about contemporary Japan. The feudal aspects of this latter group are still evident. The virtual caste system of Japanese society is the backdrop against which his dramas are played, and if this is a valid representation of current Japanese society then there is nothing wrong that it exists in Kurosawa's films. However, one must call into question some of the judgements that have been made of Kurosawa's films in the light of this evidence. Richie feels that Kurosawa's films are better than those of his ethical neighbours such as Ichikawa and Kobayashi – and on most artistic criteria they certainly are – but Richie enters the court of argument with ethical evidence, stating that Kurosawa's characters are greater humanist creations since they have this interaction with their environment. But this is to compare apples with oranges. In effect what Richie is doing is to transfer aesthetic criteria into an ethical argument, defining his terms in such a way that they will support his case. This inductive form of argument is difficult to substantiate. To be sure the central characters of Kobayashi and Ichikawa do not exist within such a well-delineated social milieu as do the characters of

Drunken angel (Kurosawa, Toho 1948)
The essential feudalism of the master/pupil relationship which permeates contemporary cinema.

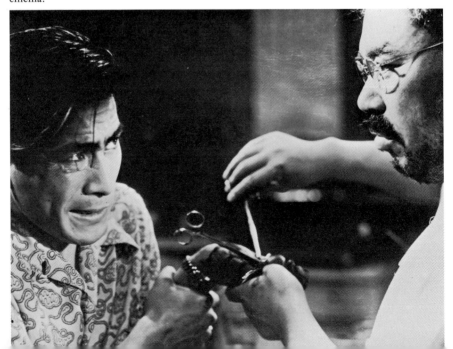

Red Beard (Kurosawa, Toho/Kurosawa Films 1965)
Kurosawa's finest expression of the apprehension of human dignity, yet formally placed within the master/pupil relationship.

Kurosawa, but they are often treated as individuals acting and living as single entities, making their own decisions and learning by their own experience. A close regard for the central characters within Kurosawa's world will show that in every case there is a relationship which is in essence feudal. The master-pupil situation, one in which values of humanist tendencies are slowly absorbed by the pupil through observation of the master, is central to each of the films culminating in what is probably Kurosawa's greatest film, *Red beard*.

Set in the Tokogawa period, this long and beautifully formulated film tells of the painful education of a proud young doctor who is sent to work under the guidance of the fierce 'Red beard' (Toshiro Mifune) in a public hospital instead of getting the more socially acceptable job at court. Here the master-pupil relationship is given its most perfect statement. In this film, with its almost isometric construction, one can see that logical working out of all the relationships both great and small that we have seen in Kurosawa's previous films. It is almost as though we were watching his final statement. This may account to some extent for the long delay before Kurosawa made another film, and why that particular film *Dodes' ka-den* (1970) lacked the power and cohesive force that the world had come to expect from such a great artist.

It would be idle speculation to look for any connection between the apparent completion of a life's work and Kurosawa's attempted suicide, but there is a parallel in the death of Yukio Mishima and the subsequent suicide of the Nobel Prize-winner, Yasunari Kawabata.

His feudal message completed, all he had left were the fascinating but smaller relationships between the poor people of the Tokyo shanty town.

Dodes' ka-den (Kurosawa, Yonki-no-Kai 1970)
A diffuse exploration of the lives of shanty-town dwellers.

No longer was there the learning process of *Sanshiro sugata*, the feudal conflict of *Rashomon*, the dying Watanabe for whom to provide a figure of the night as a guide and mentor, the high and low with the desire to discover how each other lived. Kurosawa had made his message clear that all men were brothers and were each other's responsibility, but at the same time he had made it clear that such humanistic concern could only grow to fulfillment in a world in which there were those who would be the leaders, the teachers. He seems to see man as essentially weak needing to gain moral and ethical strength through the strength of others. It is a world whose society can only exist if there are those differences which make one man the master and another the pupil.

Such an ethical posture is perfectly tenable, but in the terms of the thesis of this book it means that we must revaluate the position of Kurosawa. He is without doubt one of the great film directors, equal in stature to Ozu though different in character. To question Donald Richie's judgement that Kurosawa is the greatest humanist of the Japanese cinema is in no way to detract from Kurosawa's undoubted genius, it is only to point out that there are other film-makers who have a clearer regard for the individual in Japanese society, the individual free from the constraints of a feudal relationship.

There are two major film-makers who stand out clearly amongst even the greatest of all Japanese film-makers as men who have an abiding concern for the sanctity of the individual human being, the real champions of the ethical left, namely Kon Ichikawa and Masaki Kobayashi. The work of both these

84

directors has been of a less consistent quality over the years than that of Ozu, Mizoguchi or Kurosawa, but the degree of control held by the major Japanese studios is high and there have been few directors in the Japanese film industry who have had a free choice of projects. It is only in very recent years that either Ichikawa or Kobayashi gained production freedom and thus one finds in their work films which they might not have undertaken had they had a free choice. Not that either of them has been cowed by this experience, Ichikawa least of all, for he has been known to accept a project and then proceed to give the studio as rough a ride as they thought they were going to give him. It is even reported that the film *An Actor's revenge* was affectionately known in the business as *Ichikawa's revenge*.

Kon Ichikawa began his career in the thirties as an animator with the J.O. Studios in Tokyo. Having been trained in Western Art this was not a surprising place to find him, yet he is one of the few people in any country to make the jump from the cartoonist's drawing board to the director's chair. Working with the Toho Company he made a puppet film based on a Kabuki play, *The Girl at Dojo temple* (1945–46), and then, as mentioned previously, had to suffer the indignity of having it banned by the Americans not because of what the film said but simply because he had failed to submit the script to the censor's office before commencing production. So, in 1947, he made his public début with a hodge-podge film entitled *One thousand and one nights with Toho*.

Through the rest of the forties and the early fifties he made a steady flow of melodramas and comedies and it was not until *The Burmese harp* (1956) that film viewers outside Japan began to take notice of the new power emerging on the cinematic scene. The importance of this film is well known in terms of its pacifist attitudes, but it is also important in that it marks a watershed in the work of Ichikawa. From this point on he maintained a concern with the individual and, as Philip Strick put it in a recent review, '. . . the fine distinction between individualism and self-centredness'. This concern for the existence of the self has remained at the centre of his succeeding films. The consistency of thematic concern has not been matched by one style, so that, in truth, he could be said to have been consistently inconsistent. He has thus aroused critical suspicion by his unwillingness to be pigeonholed as a maker of any one type of film. The assumption that an artist is a better artist because he produces work that bears an individual stamp is generally accepted as a critical criterion and such a distinguishing characteristic is usually sought in the formal structure and surface texture in a film. In the case of Ichikawa that individuality can be better seen in the concern for the central character and the way in which the artistic style, whilst changing from film to film, has in each case a remarkable internal logic and consistency derived from its particular subject.

The focus that Ichikawa appears to have found in 1956 grew from a personal conviction about humanity but surfaced in his work within the context of contemporary attitudes. In the post-war era Japanese films tended to criticize old Japanese ways rather than celebrate the new ones of the Allies, but in a defeated country – where the concept of defeat was impossible – in a country on whom the appalling devastation of the atomic bomb had been released, it is not surprising that attitudes towards the military were confused. Inevitably, guilt for the involvement in the war began to creep into films, but also inevitably, it was not long before criticism against the Allied occupying forces grew like fresh bamboo. At first this criticism was subtle and oblique, frequently couched in domestic dramas, but as the fifties progressed, the bitterness felt by the Japanese towards the Americans became more

85

overt. Together with this protest came the equal and opposite reaction. Naruse, Imai and Sekigawa raged against the war and the military ethos, only thinly disguising it in war-time love stories. With the final withdrawal of American censorship in the late fifties opinion and expression became more extreme. Sekigawa, who up to this point had been a 'humanist' of sorts, made his shattering film *Hiroshima* (1953; parts of it appeared in Alain Resnais' *Hiroshima mon amour*), in which he overtly blamed the Americans for the Japanese tragedy.

However, it was not until Kon Ichikawa suddenly abandoned his specialization in domestic comedies that a direct criticism of Japan's militarism appeared on the screen. Ichikawa was one of the first directors to react to the release in Japan in 1949 of *Paisa* and *La Grande illusion* (the latter having been banned in pre-war days). These two films received respectively the first and second 'Best One' *Kinema Jumpo* awards for the year and had the effect of reinforcing Japan's official promise never again to interest herself in war. The initial anti-war films were essentially non-political. There was no big message, only an exposure of the horrors of war. But it was not long before anti-war films began to acquire a political direction and even propagandist manipulation. Yamamoto in *Vacuum zone* (1952) had exposed the brutality and corruption of the Japanese Army in its most revolting form, criticizing the abuse of power rather than militarism itself. A divergence soon developed within the anti-war genre, some taking the view that, whilst war itself was bad, men like the Kamikaze pilots acting within their code of honour were themselves noble. Others attempted to demonstrate that the military powers were fully aware of the brutality and corruption and had virtually condoned it.

Most of the many war films of the fifties were frank exploitation pictures. Many used second-rate American actors and off-duty servicemen to play the

Hiroshima (Sekigawa, PCL 1953)
Shocking reconstruction of the national tragedy used as a political weapon.

Vacuum zone (Yamamoto, Shinsei 1952)
Torture and trial in Yamamoto's exposure of military corruption.

'bad guys', and in the late fifties there was a growth of nostalgia for the war, some films being advertised, such as *Blitzkrieg operation no. 11*, not as a record of Japan's defeat in the Pacific war but as a record of the glorious victories of the Army, Navy and Air Force: '. . . See the brave deeds of your fathers and sons. Free stills from any scene in which your relatives and friends appear. War-wounded admitted free'. Films like *Kamikaze* showed the battles in detail but did not mention the desperation that had made Kamikaze possible, nor did they question the system which called for suicide squadrons. But amongst all these films there were exceptions and again one returns to the work of Kon Ichikawa. When released in Europe and America, *The Burmese harp* won critical acclaim and came at the vanguard of a rising swell of pacifist feeling around the world. Basically it is a simple story of a young Japanese soldier who is captured and then ordered to negotiate the surrender of another troop of infantry who are holed up in a cave. Both sides exhibit destructive pride and as a result the mission fails. Left as the only survivor the young man makes for the coast to join the rest of his unit. The sight of so many dead littering the countryside and the jungle paths slowly turns his anxiety for his own plight into a conviction that he must make a restitution to humanity for the inhumanity of war. Shaving his head and donning the saffron robe of a Buddhist monk he resolves to bury the dead. His action is not seen as a grand heroic gesture by the director but as a quiet and moving human choice. He faces constant doubt as to the relevance of what he is doing and the thought of returning to his homeland acts in direct conflict with his actions. Twice he struggles with the opportunity of joining his former colleagues as they search for him, and in the end he faces them across the boundary wire of the prison camp from which they will be repatriated.

With its delicate control of pace and light the film itself has the feeling of a lyric poem. None of the characters seems obtrusive, which serves to throw the actual subject of the film into a sharp if strange contrast. As a quiet unheroic treatment of war it is filled with moments of stark beauty. As the Allied forces advance on a village in which the Japanese company are hiding they start to sing 'Auld Lang Syne' – the war is over. As they realize this the Japanese troops join in the quiet singing and slowly the two groups of men walk towards each other, all reason for killing gone. Songs play a major part in this film since the young soldier/priest sings sad songs accompanying himself on a Burmese harp and it is through these songs that the soldiers eventually recognize their former colleague. It is also with a song that he takes leave of the soldiers crowded against the wire and fades back into the morning mists. It is difficult not to be totally moved by the long sequence at the end of the film as the troop commander on the boat which is taking the soldiers back to a defeated Japan reads a long letter from the monk explaining the reasons for his action. Such a film had a profound effect upon Japanese audiences who found this plea for individuality strange and disturbing.

Ichikawa was to disturb them even more with another blow to the Japanese sense of identity in the national war-machine. *Fires on the plain* (1959) is perhaps the most uncompromising statement ever made in the cinema of what war can do to the individual human being. Set in the Philippines during the final stages of the rout of the Japanese forces it traces the story of one soldier. The order and precision of the Army has been blown apart and chaos is spreading through the ranks. In every direction columns of smoke rise into the air from the fires on the plain which signal the presence of guerilla forces. Officers try to organize small parties but they break up or are destroyed. One has a sense of the army straggling across the countryside like a retreating amoeba. The 'hero' joins a number of different groups and watches the degeneration of human values as order dissipates. Everything in which he believes is challenged, all his accepted criteria for making judgements are shown to be useless in this situation. The honour and glory of a nation evaporates leaving only the personal problem of staying alive. In such a situation the vainglorious suicide becomes no choice at all, but is simply ludicrous. In horror we watch once upright soldiers kill and rob each other and eventually resort to cannibalism to stay alive. Stripped of all his points of reference the 'hero' has to decide for himself what to do, and he becomes for a time as bad as most of the others that he meets. Ichikawa manages to create hard images that jolt along in a brutal rhythm, so that the audience witnesses the horror of personal degradation through the eyes of the soldier. There is a great sense of sympathy and compassion for all men in war but Ichikawa is careful not to let the audience develop any form of romantic empathy with his characters. He calls for understanding rather than pity. To show the Japanese troops in such a situation was shocking enough for his audiences, but to show that all the values that uphold Japanese society are futile in a situation such as that was even harder to take. Few people can ever forget the end of the film as he walks forward through the rain to give himself up to the enemy rather than die. He walks forward to surrender, not knowing if he will be shot, and – what is even more horrific – no longer really caring. That he is cut down by a guerilla's bullet adds to the irony and was Ichikawa's addition to the original script.

opposite: *The Burmese harp* (Ichikawa, Nikkatsu 1956)
A search for personal identity through deliberate isolation from national identity.

Conflagration (Ichikawa, Daiei 1958)
In order to remove the Golden Temple from an unworthy world, he must destroy that which he loves.

Fires on the plain (Ichikawa, Daiei 1959)
Ichikawa's stunning version of Shohei O-oka's novel of personal enlightenment through human degradation.

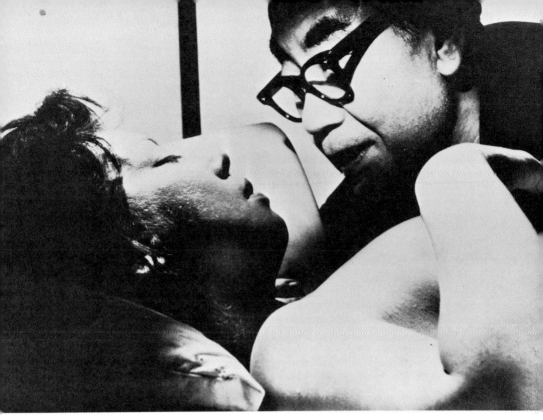

The Key (Ichikawa, Daiei 1959)
A clinical examination of deviant behaviour, filled with tolerance and understanding.

Conflagration (1958), from the novel *Enjo* by Yukio Mishima, recreates the incident in which a young acolyte set fire to the Golden Pavilion, the Kinka-kuji, in Kyoto. The cinematography (by Kazuo Miyagawa), would alone set this film high in the artistic rankings of world cinema. Using the wide screen, as it had never been used before and has rarely been used since, Ichikawa used the architecture of the temple to generate startling compositions, often squeezing characters into corners with great textured blocks of building in very sharp monochrome. Such is the quality of his images that many people felt the film was too cold and calculating, too dispassionate to get close to the character of the young man who was driven to destroy what he loved. It is noticeable that many critics, including Richie, have since modified their position as it has become clear that Ichikawa made the surface texture of the film match exactly the feelings of the central character as he finds the world around him cold and evil, a world unworthy of having the temple. It was with this film that Ichikawa fully developed his ability to blend all the elements of the film to the subject in hand rather than seek a personal style. In the same way that the entomologist studies his specimen we study this one person and begin to understand his motives. We learn a little of how each human being manages to survive independently of the social and behavioural rules.

The Key (1959), sometimes distributed as *Odd obsession*, differs from the other films of this period in that there are four central characters under close scrutiny rather than a single subject. Despite this the story of a complex family relationship in which the sexual partnerships between father and mother, daughter and doctor fiancé, doctor and mother, are exposed to each other is consistent with the oeuvre. The almost clinical examination of the deviant sexual habits is erotic in content but never in treatment. Sympathy and understanding of varying human needs, however strange, characterize the director's approach in this remarkably claustrophobic and strangely beautiful film.

After a number of films in which the central character was each time faced with a set of circumstances which removed him from the protecting norms of society, Ichikawa was given a dreadful subject for a film. *Yukinojo henge* (1963), known alternatively as *The revenge of Yukinojo* or *An Actor's revenge*, was based on an old melodrama, a work far beneath the calibre of a man like Ichikawa. Together with his wife Natto Wada, who has written all his scripts, and the two great old men of Japanese cinema, Daisuke Ito and Teinosuke Kinugasa, he reshaped the whole script, making a virtue of necessity. To be more exact, he took the old melodrama and worked it into a masterpiece. The casting of the long-popular matinée idol, Kazuo Hasegawa, as an *onnagata* of the Kabuki theatre opposite one of the most popular and beautiful young stars, Ayako Wakao, resulted in the disturbing sight of a man playing a woman making love to a woman less than half his age. The *frisson* derived from this is nothing to the startling effects that Ichikawa managed to squeeze out of the wide-screen photography. Location shooting is happily mixed with the most obvious stage sets derived from the Kabuki. It was as if someone had suddenly discovered colour and the tricks of the camera all over again. One is left with memories of brilliant sword play in the near dark from a 'woman' who never takes on male attributes even when slaying, a rope stretching off into the dark to lasso a fleeing enemy suddenly going taut and pointing off into nothing as it finds its mark. For sheer magic it has hardly been surpassed yet at its heart there is a story of a lone search for reason along a road paved with doubts. Ichikawa must have enjoyed himself making the film, to judge by the result; Daiei, the production company, were less happy since the film lost money.

The Sin (Ichikawa, Daiei 1961)
Ichikawa's attack on the intolerance of the Japanese caste system.

An Actor's revenge (Ichikawa, Daiei 1963)
Kazuo Hasegawa as Ichikawa's colourful and extravagant *onnagata*.

The concern with the single individual reached its zenith in *Alone on the Pacific* (1963), based on the true story of Kenichi Horie who sailed alone across the Pacific from Osaka to San Francisco in ninety-four days. Here the wide screen is employed to full effect again and the concentration of theme and action is total. Slipping out of the harbour one night against the wishes of his parents and the advice of his friends Horie takes the viewer with him on a voyage which is much more than the crossing of a great sea. It is as much a voyage into his own inner space as a physical challenge. By the judicious use of flashback we are slowly provided with the background that has driven the young student to this drastic step. Crushing blacks force the wide frame of the screen onto the family groups as Kenichi attempts to justify his project; the foreground is cluttered with redundant machinery in the father's workshop as he talks to his son and fails to understand why the son does not want to work in such a place. Father and son are pushed to the edges of the wide screen as they finally disagree. Once the boat is at sea the images alternate between the superbly liberated shots of the small boat on a great expanse of ocean and the interior which is even more cramped than the home that he has left.

The contrast between industrial Japan and the free sailor is far from simplistic. Horie is not fleeing a mechanized world, for it is in another such world that he arrives, but a world in which his life is predetermined, a life in which he has no choice. The very act of setting out is an affirmation of his determination to act as an individual. Ichikawa is careful to show that his hero is far from heroic. Despite his preparations he is ill-prepared, and is seasick and terrified in storms and typhoons. Full of human weakness he makes mistakes. Cooking with beer causes an explosion, he fails to see that there are sharks when he goes swimming and bashfully retreats below decks to change his shorts though hundreds of miles from the nearest human. At times of stress he has the hallucination that another self, solid and independent, is on the boat with him with whom he debates his problems. By externalizing the process of rationalization in this way Ichikawa has made one of the most positive statements about the man of the ethical left that has come out of the Japanese cinema. It is a song of praise for the existence of the self sprung from a system which tends to work against such an attitude. The shout of joy as the small boat sails under the Golden Gate Bridge into San Francisco is a cry of triumph for the liberation of the soul. Knowing that he must return to his parents, now giving enthusiastic and proud press interviews, he can choose to sleep rather than answer the telephone in the American hotel. The final shots state that his action has done nothing to change the world but we know that it has changed and freed him.

Such an affirmation is multiplied in *Tokyo Olympiad* (1965). Using a battery of cameramen Ichikawa has made a hymn of praise to the human spirit. Some critics have compared this film with Leni Riefenstahl's *Olympische Spiele* (1936) and have found it wanting. They seem to be disappointed that it is not as 'poetic', or that it does not glorify athletes enough. Perhaps they are looking for the wrong thing. In the light of the rest of his work it is not surprising to find that his version of the Olympic Games is not really a film about athletics. He does not see teams and nations striving for prizes and glory, he looks with compassion on a vast collection of individual human beings striving to conquer their own limitations. Riefenstahl sees the athletes as beautiful sculptures, breaking down bodies into gleams of light from glistening muscles, lyrical flows of mixed images creating a glittering panoply of splendour. Where Riefenstahl captures the concept of the supreme athlete

Tokyo Olympiad (Ichikawa, Toho 1965)
National identity superseded by Ichikawa's concentration on the individual struggling against his own limitations.

Ichikawa seeks out and finds the fallible human being. From the start of the film he uses the camera to disclose the feelings and emotions of the people involved. He throws the torch carriers back into the landscape so that they become scarcely moving plumes of smoke, the long lens probes through the crowds to find an old man crying. Every composition seems to lead the viewer towards an empathy for the human behind the athlete. Crammed to one side of the wide screen is a sprinter waiting in the blocks to explode into the empty space spread out in front of us; slow motion makes the waiting an agony and we share the tense build-up before the gun as muscles writhe instead of twitching. Freeze-framing momentarily reveals the powerful shot-putting women as people suffering extreme pain through effort. By refusing to concentrate on the big stars and the glamour events Ichikawa shifts the attention from the medals to the endeavours. Often we see the losers rather than the winner for to Ichikawa they are as important as those in the limelight. Having watched the Japanese girls win the gold medal for the volley-ball contest, a contest of bodies which rise, fall, and spin back off the shining floor with balletic ease, he slides his camera away from the moment of glory to look at the team coach standing by himself. Slowly he sits down and puts his head in his hands, all effort expended, all strength gone.

Most famous of all is the final nineteen-minute sequence of the marathon. Developing from a gripping montage of running feet and bobbing heads Ichikawa gradually singles out Abebe Bikila as he steadily forges ahead. Fatigue takes its toll as one after another runner drops out, yet even these are treated with respect and sympathy by the camera. Soon it becomes apparent that there is only one man in the race and the sound fades to isolate the Ethiopian in his quiet contest against his own body. Strain shows in the long face as it weaves in slow motion past a blurred crowd and one has a sense of the intense loneliness of the man out in the front.

Full of humour and moments of stark beauty this film must surely stand as one of the great statements on the dignity of man. Such a personal vision was not calculated to please the Games Committee. At Cannes, he reported the misgivings of these gentlemen, who would obviously have preferred a newsreel. 'They even asked whether I could re-shoot some of it, but I was able to reply truthfully that circumstances prevented it as the entire cast had left Japan'.

In an interview in *Sight and Sound* (Summer 1970) Ichikawa was asked why, since the completion of *Tokyo Olympiad*, he had only worked on documentaries and television serials:

'It is necessary to have a stable world to make good fiction films; there is a weakness in the arts now but I feel better times are coming. ... For me *Conflagration* was the turning point. Then I realized what film-making really meant and became more objective. Life should be viewed from further away. ... You know, contemporary French cinema (except Bresson) has made the whole world bad.'

11 Kobayashi: champion of revolt

The Sudden Sorrow

Cutting through my body:
In our bedroom, I tread on
My dead wife's comb.

Taniguchi Buson 1715–1783

The work of Masaki Kobayashi does not have the same sense of focus as that of Kon Ichikawa. It is not easy to see any thematic or intellectual link running through his work as a whole, yet he remains one of the major talents of the Japanese cinema and certainly one of the most powerful spokesmen of the ethical left wing.

Having served as an apprentice to Keisuke Kinoshita, Masaki Kobayashi began directing films in 1952. It is perhaps fortunate that amongst his best films, the ones that have had foreign distribution, should be those which most strongly express a critical attitude towards the conventions of social behaviour within Japanese society. From the beginning of his career he has made periodic sallies against the bastions of conventionalism, questioning the Japanese social conscience. One of his earliest films *I'll buy you* (1956) concerned the shameless goings-on in the midst of Japan's national sport, baseball. Since it was close to well-known cases of corruption the public reaction was considerable. His critical position was reaffirmed in the following year by *Black river* (1957) which centred on the whores and gangsters who were setting up around the US military bases throughout Japan. The style of the film is detached and objective, making no overt judgement on the 'hostesses', yet by its detached observations of a taboo subject it stands as an indictment of the social system which generates such behaviour and at the same time tries to ignore its growth. The boldness of this statement was bound to be followed by reaction but since it enjoyed good box-office returns Kobayashi was allowed to proceed with an epic film which in its scope and grandeur restored the meaning to the word 'epic'.

In its original version *Ningen no joken* parts I-III (1959–61) ran for a staggering nine hours and thirty-nine minutes. In Japan it was issued in three parts: *No greater love, Road to eternity* and *A Soldier's prayer*. Overseas it was issued under a number of titles, the most common of which was *The Human condition*. As *Barfuss durch die Holle* it broke the German post-war box-office records. Yet all of the export versions of this master work were severely cut down from the original and as a result do not retain the epic sweep and the shocking rhythms as action bursts out from long lyric passages. The effect of the film and its importance to the world of the cinema does not

96

lie in any claim to be the longest feature film, but in its subject matter and the treatment of the central character.

Based on the novel by Jumpei Gomikawa the film tells the story of Kaji (played to perfection by Tatsuya Nakadai). As a labour supervisor for the South Manchurian Steel Company he sees the injustices of the treatment of the workers, especially the prisoners of war, and attempts to help them. His actions, which are necessarily contrary to the wishes of the establishment, produce suspicion from both the managers and the workers. He slowly becomes a man outside the system, fighting it from an impossible position. He is then suddenly called up and sent to the front without even being given the chance to see his wife. The second part concerns itself with the conflict between Kaji, who sees himself acting as a humane socialist, and the Army authorities who have been warned that he might be a Communist. Army life is shown as unbearably cruel – and here the film probes relentlessly the Japanese military mind and practice. Eventually these poorly-equipped and underfed soldiers have to face the Soviet tanks with nothing more than rifles to defend themselves. Slaughter ensues but Kaji survives to gather together the survivors of the bloody and futile fight.

The third and final part tells of the flight south ahead of the advancing Soviet Army, filled with all the horrors that the human being is capable of committing. One of the party suggests surrender but Kaji rejects this, not for the normal reason that surrender is unthinkable to a Japanese, for these men have long lost such illusions, but in order to go on and find the wife he was forced to leave. Eventual capture thwarts his hopes. Once again Kaji is placed in a situation in which he fights against authority. He pleads for a

The Human condition: No greater love (Kobayashi, Shochiku 1959)
The individual's confrontation with established authority. Passive resistance becomes active aggression.

more humane treatment of the prisoners and in response is punished with hard labour. Now he has to re-examine his affection for the socialist system. The underlying point is that Kaji sees that when the beliefs he holds to become ossified into a system, become dogmas, they lose their humanity. Determined to beat the system and to find his wife Kaji escapes, but weakened by privation he eventually sinks to the ground and is covered by the falling snow.

To kill off the hero in this way gave the whole epic a more tragic aspect in retrospect since all his efforts fail against a system shown as evil or at the least flawed; but the pessimism of the final moments in no way detracts from the more positive criticisms raised throughout this magnificent work. Gone was the restrained objectivity of the earlier films, the attack was as raw and hard as the image quality that conveyed the message. In many ways this was a revolutionary film. There had been films of social complaint before but they were like whining boys compared to this roar. Kobayashi had stood up and shouted that not only did we do all these things wrong, but that there is no justification for any system, social, commercial or military, to impose its will upon the individual. Where Kurosawa sees the right of the individual as the right to adopt the values of those about him, to reassess them and to learn how to co-exist with other men, Kobayashi sees it as the right of the individual to act without the rigid strictures of an imposed order and if he finds the system wanting then to change it. Where Ichikawa sees the duty of the individual as being the need to reason out his own course of action, Kobayashi goes further. Not only should the individual decide his own course of action but he should also act positively against those elements of society which dictate the status quo. This is far from being a simple cry for the removal of all authoritarian structures, for there is little of the anarchist in his work. In each of his films in which a character does act against a social or military body the impetus for this action is a concern for the treatment of others. Kaji tries to improve the lot of the workers and the prisoners, and in so doing exposes the failings within each of the governing structures.

Kobayashi began to emerge as a spokesman against the absolute acceptance of the traditional, and perhaps his most daring step was the making of what was released in the West as *Harakiri* (1962). This stands as one of the strongest of all anti-feudal statements. It is a pity that the distributors found it necessary to use the title of *Harakiri* since this really denotes 'belly-cutting' and was fostered by Japan's wartime enemies as a derogatory term for the act of ritual suicide. The original title of *Seppuku* conveys the ritual and spiritual aspect of this strange act and has all the right connotations of the Samurai clan and its *bushido* code.

Harakiri tended to be regarded, when first released in the West, as simply a superb if rather gruesome piece of sword play. But it has a more serious aspect. In fact its humanistic view of the cold intricacies of Tokogawa feudalism was a passionately concerned view. The same aspect was being considered at the same time by Kurosawa, who took the *Jidai-geki* towards high comedy in *Sanjuro*. Both directors were attacking the mentality that had resulted from Japan having been a police state for six hundred years. The question they put was: 'What do you do about it now?' Nor did Kobayashi reserve his attack on feudalism for the period film. In 1962 he made *The Inheritance*, which was seen by many as simply a film about the difference between the generations. But the attack is still on the feudal attitudes of old Japan though in a contemporary setting. In *Harakiri* Kobayashi takes care to acknowledge the virtues of the strong clan system of the samurai and its codes of honour so that the distortions of the code can also be seen. Set in a time of peace when many samurai found themselves without work, the film is a study of the corrupting influence of power and ossified tradition. Using a brilliant narrative structure of complex flash-backs Kobayashi tells the tale of Hanshiro Tsugumo who arrives at the clan house asking to be allowed to commit *seppuku* – a common occurrence at that time, as the claimant was often given alms or employment rather than have him go through with the act on one's own premises. The clan leader tries to discourage Hanshiro with the tale of Motome Chijiiwa who was forced by the clan to go through with the ritual even though he had sold his blades in order to eat and had to kill himself with bamboo blades. Kobayashi's camera dwells on the excruciating death of the young man, not from any love of horror but to drive home his message about the stupidity of the feudal codes.

Hanshiro then reveals that Motome was his son-in-law. And at this point, crucial in the structure of the film, one man's search for vengeance against those individuals whom he believed responsible for the needless death of Motome turns into an all-out attack on the clan itself. An important aspect of this film is the way Kobayashi handles the fights. The plot itself is well suited to *chambara*, the normal blood-and-thunder treatment, yet Kobayashi avoids any gross gesture, any theatrical effect. By creating the exact style of the fighting masters he elevates the action of the film to an artistic ritual. The starkness of these ritual elements is impressed upon the viewer during Motome's suicide. Kobayashi's high-angle camera isolates the white square set on an expanse of raked sand, round which in a regular pattern are set the members of the samurai clan. The details of the ritual are carefully observed, since it is necessary to establish the calm order of this ceremony with its terrible action at the centre in order to appreciate the effect of Hanshiro's action.

The sight of Hanshiro sitting in the middle of the courtyard takes on a new significance once we have seen the flashback to Motome. Now we are aware

Harakiri (Kobayashi, Shochiku 1962)
Attacking a feudal order from within its own code, Hanshiro turns personal revenge into a destructive attack on outdated tradition.

of his overt intentions yet we can see that he is confident and smiling. The inherent contradiction in this scene is made clear to us as we are shown why the three people that have been requested by Hanshiro as seconds for his *seppuku* are not present. Here Kobayashi strikes a well-judged contrast with the geometric rigidity of the court scenes as we are shown each of the fights in which Hanshiro cut off the sacred top-knot from the warriors of the clan whom he considered to be responsible for the death of his son-in-law. A fight in the windblown grass amongst the grave-stones has rightly become famous. Composition, camera movement, action and sound all combine to make a film equivalent of the highest form of martial art. The way in which the combatants face off against each other, hardly moving for long moments, is a near-perfect expression of the concept that a fight is won before the sword has left the scabbard – physical action is superseded by mental conflict. Stillness suddenly exploding into action, handled as brilliantly as anything in Kurosawa, places the audience in the same position as Shimura in *The Seven samurai*, when watching the braggart's challenge to the swordsman. We too are asked to look at both protagonists and then shake our heads as we realize that there is no real contest. Only one solution is possible, Hanshiro must win. These fights perform much more than a simple narrative function for they make clear the fact that Hanshiro is not just attacking the inhumanity of the clan system but that he has himself become one of the best exponents of that system's fighting form. He is attacking the whole system from within its walls.

There is a deadly logic in Hanshiro's actions which result in the inevitable battle between one man and the rest of the clan. This can be seen as an act of sacrifice which exposes the weaknesses of the *bushido* code to the outside world – by destroying one clan he forces examination of all the others. The fight which ends the film is wonderful in its balletic control. Hanshiro fights with all the expertise of a grand master, striking down opponents without even looking directly at them. His ability, learned through that very clan system, creates chaos out of the empty meaningless order.

In this apocalyptic vision of man the destroyer, Kobayashi has been careful to balance his judgement of humanity. *Harakiri* is an angry and violent film calling for the serious questioning of all authoritarian systems, yet in the final moments his hero is cut down by the advances of technology. Being a product of that system he has no defences against the new muskets – and falling wounded he invokes the final irony of the film when he conforms to his samurai code by disembowelling himself with his own sword. Man may fight against a system but he cannot escape being part of it. The Japanese, he appears to be saying, must look to their own social structure yet they must at all times remember they are Japanese and carry with them the cultural history of their nation.

The visual quality that characterized *Harakiri*, beautifully composed still set pieces intercut with outbursts of action matched by a flowing camera, is further developed in *Rebellion* (*Joi-uchi*, 1967). From the first focus-pull from the leading edge of a new sword to the impassive face of the samurai who is to test it ceremoniously on a straw dummy, the film maintains a remarkable control of the scope screen and the full range of monochrome tones. Kazuo Yamada's photography frames the characters in the formal patterns of the Japanese mansion, matching perfectly the formal manner of a leading samurai who is still one of the vassals of Lord Matsudaira, then smoothly slides into tracking shots which prowl round some dramatically explosive action. Like *Harakiri*, *Rebellion* is set in feudal times and tells of one man's attack on the code of feudal rule and the submission of the individual to the wish of the ruling lord. In a truly magnificent performance

Toshiro Mifune created the character of Sasahara the leader of the samurai clan. Using all his screen stature Mifune made this samurai into a fully rounded being, full of silent strength yet completely human. Two actions are shown in slow-paced detail; firstly Matsudaira foists his cast-off mistress on Sasahara's eldest son Yogoro. There is no question of choice in this, they have to obey, but good emerges as genuine love blossoms between the two young people. Secondly Sasahara decides to retire as leader and hand over the reins of power to his son, who, by now, has been blessed with a daughter, Tomi. The calm beauty of a series of compositions convey with a minimum of words the love that stabilizes this family relationship.

Up to this point there appears to be nothing remarkable about the story, unless one has noted the extent of Sasahara's human rather than formal character. The point of rebellion arises from the decision of Lord Matsudaira to take back the Lady Ichi. Faced with a situation in which they would normally have to comply without question Sasahara and his family decide that too much is involved. The love that the members of the family have for each other seems to be of greater importance than subservience to their recognized lord.

Kobayashi is not here saying that the family is important over all other things. He reasons that human love and a sense of personal duty are above the unthinking response to a feudal command. For an individual to act in this way, to challenge the complete basis of a social system, is shocking to the Japanese. Sasahara takes over the control of the clan once more, and contradicts almost every code on which he had been raised by deciding to defy the whole of authority. The death of his son and daughter-in-law in the first fight is not really unexpected. What is unusual is that Sasahara wins in his fight against the rest of the clan, for at that time such an outcome would not

Rebellion (Kobayashi, Toho/Mifune 1967)
Sasahara finds a new answer to the conflict between duty and personal feeling in his decision to attack the very basis of the clan structure.

Rebellion (Kobayashi, Toho/Mifune 1967)
The full significance of samurai training is captured in the moments of silence which precede the fight between two great swordsmen.

have been possible. He then sets out for the capital to tell the Shogun of the tyrannical rule of Matsudaira. At a border post he meets Tatewaki Asano, a man whom he had personally trained and who now leads the border guards. Tatewaki understands the situation but is not able to transcend what he sees as his duty. They fight and Tatewaki is killed. Sasahara's moment of victory is short as he is cut down by the bullets of the pursuing troops. The child is left sitting alone.

Such a brief description can do little to convey the extraordinary visual quality and economy of statement that fills out *Rebellion*. When the camera dwells on the domestic scenes, the peace of the vision is transmitted to the audience. Sasahara's moment of decision to oppose the whole feudal system because of his love for his family is transmitted in silence: in a high-angle shot over the courtyard we watch him walk, hands behind his back, across the ornate paths. Suddenly he turns and walks across the carefully raked sand leaving a line of footprints, as if he were walking across the face of tradition.

Humour of a black kind has a place in this film. When the wet-nurse asks why all the *tatami* (floor-mats) has been taken up and half the doors have been barred by crossed spears, Sasahara gently tells her that it is for a religious festival that they always have at this time of the year and in any case it means that his feet will not slip so much in the blood when the fighting starts. The audience is aware an attack is about to descend upon the house yet apart from these strange preparations we know little of the fighting skill of

Sasahara. Kobayashi shows us in a single gesture. Hearing the approach of the enemy, Sasahara draws his sword in one swift clean movement and takes the top off the candle, plunging the room into darkness. The battle that follows outdoes even *Harakiri*. The sight of Mifune cutting, turning and crashing through paper walls has rarely been equalled. Such a fight has all the elements of the old Ito films, which led to a debased form of melodramatic slashing, but here the degree of control and skill is remarkable. Every movement is calculated and minimal – a brilliant and cruel performance. Kobayashi shows a man raised to the peak of fighting skill using that very skill to destroy the system that has created it. Much the same attitude is applied to the fight at the border when all the aspects of the samurai are called into play. Tatewaki recognizes that Sasahara is the better swordsman and during the balletic manoeuvres which precede the first drawing of the swords he asks that the end be swift and clean.

In this film Kobayashi has made his most overt and powerful attack on all that can be considered feudal within Japanese society. If only for the films considered here he must be considered as a major spokesman of the ethical left. His central characters have all the individuality of those of Ichikawa, yet in common with Kurosawa he makes them operate from within the system that they are attacking. But unlike the characters of Kurosawa his refuse to accept a small contest; they are all placed in situations in which they have to take on a whole system, and the very act results in their death. Feudalism may have triumphed but its structure is so damaged that it can never be the same again. The intensity of Kobayashi's plea is difficult to ignore, but he is fighting so many centuries of tradition that it is difficult to see at the present time what effect he can have upon the social structure of his country. One thing remains undeniable. Kobayashi has produced some works of such shocking beauty that he must be regarded as one of the major humanists of the Japanese cinema.

If we are to regard Kurosawa, Ichikawa and Kobayashi as the spokesmen for the ethical left then one must raise the question of why these masters have not produced any work of a similar calibre in the last few years. Kurosawa appeared to complete a logical process when he made *Red beard*, while Ichikawa awaits a change in the world around him. Kobayashi continues to make feature films and there is much hope that he will speak again with his powerful voice. His work has been inconsistent in its target and the Japanese cinema could still benefit from the strength of this brilliant opponent of complacency. Since the middle sixties the torch seems to have passed from this generation of film-makers – now it is in the hands of the more radical young (or at least those young by the standards of the Japanese movie industry). Whatever happens in the next few years the world has already recognized the greatness of Ozu, Naruse, Gosho, Mizoguchi, Kurosawa, Ichikawa and Kobayashi and in this sense they can be regarded as the 'old school'. Their influence is felt throughout the Japanese cinema.

The long period during which these directors have been making films has seen many genuine creative talents in the Japanese cinema and one is only too well aware that such a brief survey as this does a great injustice to these men by their very omission. Men such as Kinugasa, Imamura, Imai and many others stand out as major directors within this prolific industry and are worthy of study in themselves. This section has attempted to outline briefly the ethical spectrum that runs across the Japanese cinema by a consideration

High and low (Kurosawa, Toho/Kurosawa Films 1963)
The physical and intellectual barrier between industrialists and kidnapper.

of some of its finest artifacts. The criteria for ethical judgement will apply equally to all other works. It is no accident that those directors who have produced work that is most obviously characteristic of a position within this ethical spectrum are also those who have produced the work of the highest aesthetic virtue. It may be a dangerous generalization but it seems fair to suggest that those artists with the greatest expressive skill within the cinema are also those with clearly defined attitudes both towards the society in which they live and to their fellow men.

Part three
Eros and massacre

12 Introduction

Modern Senryu

European food
Every blasted plate
Is round.

Translated by:
Geoffrey Bownas and
Anthony Thwaite

Because they produce more films in a single language than anybody else it follows that the Japanese will also produce more bad films than anyone else. Lying behind the top quality work are vast numbers of banal, melodramatic and over-sentimental potboilers.

Eros plus massacre (Yoshida, Gendai Eiga Sha 1969)
An eroduction based on real events blending sex and violence with left-wing political commentary.

The *haha-mono* and the *tsuma-mono* accounted for a large percentage of the poor products through the fifties, together with a constant flow of period films both sentimental and bloodthirsty. As Japanese society began to feel the reverberations of youthful change in the early sixties, the studios, recognizing a new audience, echoed such changes and turned much of their production over to *yakuza* or gangster films. Such was the public demand for them that for a while it seemed there might be a turning point to the falling attendance figures. For the malaise that was being felt around the world struck hard in Japan. The boom of the post-war years with its almost unbelievable rate of increase in the number of cinemas was at an end. Costs of production rose causing an inevitable rise in the cost of cinema admissions. Television burgeoned and fed off the huge conurbations with their advertising potential and one of the world's highest TV ownership levels. As in Hollywood film studios have moved into the production of film for television. Toei attempted to combat the pressures that they were beginning to feel by launching the most adventurous production schedule that the world has seen. But such a programme involves a company in huge financial risks and took Toei into more than one difficult patch. Not all have ridden the storms: in 1972 Daiei Motion Picture Co. Ltd were declared bankrupt.

The surviving four companies of the once 'big five' are in a much less secure position than they have ever held. Many of the leading directors who were working under the rigid contracts of the big studios have left to form their own groups, such as Yonki-no-kai (made up of Akira Kurosawa, Keisuke Kinoshita, Kon Ichikawa and Masaki Kobayashi).

The face of the industry has been radically changed in the last five years by the emergence of these independent companies. There have always been small independent groups working on the fringe but they did not have any

Sex Jack (Wakamatsu, Shibata 1970)
Brutal gangsterism with conscious cold-blooded killing.

Drifting boys (Sekigawa, PCL 1960)
Typical of the films considering the problems of youth, though mild by comparison with the later *yakuza* films.

noticeable effect until Kaneto Shindo created international interest with his film *The Naked island* (sometimes released as *The Island*, 1960). Since that time more than two hundred companies have been established in Tokyo alone.

These structural changes were not solely a result of economic pressures or attempts to avoid the paternalism of the big studios. To a large degree they resulted from a desire to make films of a more outspoken nature. Cheap gangster films filled with violence and eroticism appeared as a reflection of urban society, and were all too soon snapped up by the bigger studios. The independents broke new ground by making their films more sexually explicit. Yet again the pull of big money drew the large studios into the market and now even the television companies have moved in. While in the mid-sixties something of the order of two-thirds to three-quarters of feature production was of the gangster type, now in the early seventies this percentage has been taken over by 'eroductions' or what they call 'pink' film.

Many countries of the civilized world are facing the open exploitation of the sex and violence that already exist below the surface. For some this represents a new liberal, artistic means of expression, a sense of honesty after the repressions of the past. For others it is a gold-mine to be exploited. It is a sad comment on society when the well-motivated members of the first group are fed on by the parasites of the second causing eventually an equally prurient backlash.

Sexuality runs strongly through Japanese art and literature. Many of her greatest artists did work which the Western world would label pornographic.

Indeed Japan has existed for a long time on the happy acceptance of a double standard. Until recently it was a rare sight to see young people holding hands in public, let alone kiss, yet at the same time erotic pillow books would be given to the young bride, the art of sexual coupling was developed as in no other country, and until quite recently prostitution was a legal and licensed profession. Within the terms of Japanese society there was no real void but rather a balanced coexistence between private and public behaviour. The barriers felt in the more puritan countries could not exist in a country which has communal bathing but strict codes of public action. In recent years the cinema has seen the result of the confusion that has struck the Japanese system as a result of the imposition and inept adaptation of Western puritan ethics. Those who have grown up since the war have to balance the complex values of the past with the confusing and often irrelevant values of the present. It is not surprising therefore to find that in films of recent years there has been an increasingly specific use of sex and a close relationship between this and violence.

13 Ghosts and flashing swords

Silent, But . . .

I may be silent, but
I'm thinking.
I may not talk, but
Don't mistake me for a wall.

Tsuboi Shigeji (*b.* 1889)
Translated by:
Geoffrey Bownas and
Anthony Thwaite

Ghosts and goblins and a host of fairy-tale characters appear in the literature and story-telling traditions of most nations in this world, yet with the coming of the printed word and our technological era they have disappeared from the everyday consciousness of most countries which claim to be civilized. (The modern European horror film has more to do with the dark recesses of the Victorian gothic novel than any subculture of genuine folk myth.) Why is it then that the Orient, notably India, the East Indies, China and Japan, cling tenaciously to their traditions? The reasons are perhaps complex. In a country like India, with its widely differing ranges of technological development, one can understand the popularity of the fairy-tale within the village community, which has a low level of literacy. The same holds true of Indonesia, where the story-teller and the shadow-puppet theatre still hold strong sway in the cultural scene. But what of a modern twentieth-century country like Japan? If it had developed culturally in the same way as the Occident, one would expect the ghost tradition to be vestigial, like Celtic myth, or the modern myth development of a writer like H. P. Lovecraft. However, one can see by looking at Japanese cinema that the dead are very much alive today. Much of this is due to the strong and long-held traditional values in Japan. The story-teller and the folk drama held sway for two thousand years, and the country cannot shed this level of cultural instinct in a mere hundred years of technological development. Yet if the modern world is to wipe away the myths of the past, one would expect to see the demise of the ghost-story in Japan. However, the contrary has happened: this genre has managed to hold its place in the Japanese film.

Within Japanese cultures the regard for the dead is substantially different from our own. Whilst there is human sorrow at the passing of a loved one, as can be seen in realistic terms in *Tokyo story*, there is not the well-defined border line between the living and the dead common to occidental thought. The Japanese artist has for centuries presented the real as unreal and the unreal as real and contemporary audiences find this quite acceptable. In fact, a strongly-held belief in the reality of the dead, both in religious and psychological terms, does much to explain the presence of ghosts in Japanese films. They appear in full fleshly form so that a favourite plot tells of the dead princess or geisha who seduces, in very real terms, a manly samurai. There is however a certain ambivalence towards these ghostly figures. Whilst traditional culture and religious beliefs support a tendency to accept the unreal as an empirical fact, there is also a sense of vicarious pleasure in enjoying a good ghost story on its own terms, knowing it to be simply a fantasy.

Kobayashi's *Kwaidan* (1964), from four ghost stories by an American writer who spent most of his life in Japan, Lafcadio Hearn, is a good example of simple ghost stories told with brilliance. Recognizing that at the base of all good ghost stories lies a foundation of psychological reality, Kobayashi does not conduct a search for resounding statements on the human condition. Two of these stories contain the love between the living and the dead that is found in many Japanese films, presented in the normal manner with subtle indications rather than clearly announcing the fact. Kobayashi sets his stories in a mysterious world – half theatrical and half realistic. The anamorphic lens twists and distorts in *The Black hair*. *Woman of the snow* (shown separately in some countries) has a painted backdrop to all the outdoor scenes with a strange cloud-formation like an all-seeing eye. Here he gives a clue which would be obvious to a Japanese audience. The beautiful young woman who marries Minokichi and eventually turns out to be the snow ghost introduces herself as Yuki, a normal girl's name but also the word for snow. In *Hoichi*

Kuroneko (Shindo, Kindai Eiga Kyokai 1968)
In the all-engulfing bamboo forest, revenging female ghosts take on full corporeal reality.

the earless, Kobayashi excels himself in the sheer theatricality of cutting from a screen painting of the battle of Dannoura to a mannered and stylistic reconstruction, and the subtle changes from rotting gravestones to the statuesque court of the Minamoto.

What appears to have happened in recent years within Japanese literary and cinematic movements is an assimilation of this acceptance of ghosts into a new conceptual approach. Ghosts are used not as symbols but as representations of the psychological attitudes of the Japanese. Nowhere in Japanese literature does one find a consciously structured mythology such as Tolkien has produced; there is no need for this, since ghosts and fairies can be used within the apparent reality of narrative, either as plot function, or to elucidate a psychological state.

The period film, the natural home of myths and magic, is also the stronghold of that other essential ingredient of the genre: the samurai and his sword. Granted feudal rule, the samurai has a fully understood rôle within the period narrative developed from the popular arts of the period, the *kodan* and the *naniwa-bushi*. These are recited stories, complicated in plot and seemingly endless in number, the more famous of which the Japanese know from early childhood. This prior knowledge of the story is often assumed by the film-maker, thereby relieving himself of the need for any exposition, since it is familiarity rather than novelty which entrances a normal Japanese audience. The *kodan* stories on film often concern themselves with the undeveloped phases of the life of a well-known character. It is as if one were being given the subplot to a better known action. Of course this can cause a great deal of confusion to the non-Japanese viewer who is unlikely to know the full story to which all the references are being made. Favourite stories are naturally those filmed most often, and the hardiest of the perennials, which also appeared as a Kabuki play, is the *Loyal forty-seven Ronin* of which one or even two versions are made each year. All these period films share a majority of elements, one such being the respect for the *giri-ninjo* conflict: the battle between obligations and human feelings, the contention between duty and inclination. In the more traditional film duty always wins. Better artists do more than simply point to this conflict but expose and analyse it. Mizoguchi showed the potential of this type of film in *Shin heike monogatari* (*New tales of the Taira clan*, 1955), while Kobayashi used it to exemplify reaction at the other end of the scale in *Rebellion*. In addition to the conventions of the original stories the films have added elements as banal as the old 'western' idea that the baddy always wore a black hat and the one in the white hat was the 'goodie'.

The majority of the period films are set in the Tokogawa period, just before the reopening of the country in 1868, and generally hinge on the rivalry between the Imperial forces and the shogunate. Although history favours neither, tradition in the cinema says that the Imperial side was in the right, for in the years immediately preceding the war it would have been foolish to have suggested otherwise, and even in the post-war years this bias has remained. For the viewer who cannot recognize the sides by the flags they carry the easiest way to tell which is the Imperial army is to count those standing at the end of a battle. Such is the abandon of the sword play in these films that they are distinguished from *Jidai-geki*, which means 'period play', by the term *chambara* – a sort of gross blood-and-thunder melodrama. Donald Richie has written:

'It is nothing for one of these *chambara* heroes to kill anything from twenty-five to fifty people in one film, and all by himself. The enemy gang attacks the single hero who – if it is a musical period film – will sing whilst he slashes, missing neither note nor man.'

Love not again (Uchida, Toei 1962)
The classic quality of Uchida's period films which he has maintained since the silent days.

The demands of the film industry and television, which has its own heavy output of period films, have developed what one sees as the newest martial art – amongst the many martial arts of Japan – the highly skilled ability to fight with the sword without actually touching the opponent, but making it look, to the camera, as though one has. Apart from the better known examples of this skill, such as Mifune and Nakadai in various period rôles, there are many more deadly and exciting characters, not least of whom is Zato Ichi, a blind wandering priest whose unfailing instinct makes him miraculously powerful. A peculiar off-shoot of the period film has been the steady develop-ment of a rather gruesome form of make-up and special effect. Limbs are cut off and bodies chopped in two, all in full vision, and recently the Japanese created a method in which after a sword has apparently slashed a man's face, there is a pause for two or three seconds before the razor-sharp 'cut' opens and the blood flows. All of this arises from the predominance of violence in the Japanese film, which has as one of its main features a high rate of pointless killing, whether in a *chambara* or a *yakuza* film. Even Japanese critics such as Tadao Sato have commented that the viewer of such bloodthirsty films must soon be led inescapably to feel that life is considered cheap by Japanese film-makers. Not only are there vast numbers of killings but the details of each slaughter are lovingly observed. Long before *The Wild bunch*, *yakuza* films had flesh exploding in slow motion under the impact of bullets. Richie tells of a film in which a man falls towards the camera, fatally shot or stabbed. But that is not enough. Right in the foreground, next to the camera, he drops his head into fire. As we watch his face burn away, horses trample on his body, all in full detail. Even children's educational films showed cruelty far beyond the requirements of the plot. One expects to see the victory of justice; one does not expect to see children as ministers of that justice jumping on the captured miscreant to smash his rib cage.

Period films had a temporary flourish in the late fifties and for a time accounted for nearly a third of the production figures. They exhibit a tendency common to much of Japanese cinema to display trivial emotionalism rather than any higher tragic feeling. As has often been pointed out the Japanese drama does not have any equivalent, in terms of heightened emotion, to *King Lear* or *Phèdre*, and it is even said that they don't quite see what the fuss is about in *Hamlet* since he is simply avenging his father and loves his mother like any dutiful son should do. Such an attitude has sprung from the tradi-tional ethical right wing which regards the wishes and needs of the individual to be subservient to those of society, in most cases represented by the family unit. This is not an uncaring posture but solidly based in *mono-no-aware*.

While acknowledging that the main influence on the period film is the story-telling tradition, one must recognize the influence of Kabuki (although it is nothing like as strong as many foreign critics believe). Kabuki is a theatre of performance rather than content and many of the plays have remarkably little plot. However the period film does draw some of its strength from the classical theatre, specifically the *Kabuki aragato*, which were rough-house plays mainly concerning the exploits of famous samurai. As a genre it is full of action, huge gesture and much sword-play. Unfortunately this is the type of play that many Japanese like to show to foreigners. Tsuneo Hazumi, the film critic has said:

'Unfortunately, there has never been any real connection between Kabuki and films. The earliest period films, a poor substitute for the genuine Kabuki, were acted by rural troops which had no connection with the great Kabuki traditions, and none of its art.'

The bastard child which this admixture spawned grew to be a massive genre. In its growth it has exploited all the violence inherent in the nation's history, and today it is as gruesomely and explicitly sadistic as appears possible. There is much evidence in the young of a need for this vicarious violence, though this normally finds its outlet in the *yakuza* and 'pink' films.

Stylistically the sword-play period films were set in a mould in the earliest years of this century by Daisuke Ito. Looking at his work today is still a shock, for not only are his actors superbly skilled in the handling of the curved blade but his audacious use of the camera is startlingly modern. With a sure choreographic touch he slides his camera into furious battles, catches the essential action and pulls back again at high speed. Modern techniques have hardly improved on Ito's work.

Few directors have managed to make genuine *Jidai-geki*, genuine in terms of a physical and psychological equivalent to the spirit of the past. The majority make *chambara* devoid of content, unnecessarily brutal, banal in the extreme and yet shatteringly exciting.

14 Art, anti-art, cartoons and monsters

Tourist Japan

Fujiyama – we sell.
Miyajima – we sell.
Nikko – we sell.
Japan – we sell anywhere.
Naruto, Aso –
We sell it all.
Prease, prease, come and view!
Me rub hands,
Put on smile.
Money, money – that's the thing!
We Japanese all buy cars
We Japanese all like lighters
We Japanese all good gardeners
We Japanese all sing pops.
All of us bow,
All, all, are meek and mild. Yes!

Takenaka Iku (*b.* 1904)
Translated by:
Geoffrey Bownas
and Anthony Thwaite

The long history of art in Japan is one of high sophistication and an integration of life and nature to such an extent that it is often difficult to tell whether nature has influenced art or art nature. The gradual reduction of the number of brush strokes required to paint a picture, as in the *haboku* or 'splashed ink' technique of Sesshu (1420–1506), is symptomatic of an approach to art which rejects those elements which can be made redundant. Such is the degree of self-control in the better Japanese artists that when they reform nature in an unnatural way, the unnatural becomes natural. That the Japanese have a vision of their own, a way of seeing things distinct from that of even their near neighbours, becomes obvious after the most cursory consideration of any of their art forms. Throughout their artistic development they have tended to see nature as a form of art, and through the desire for simplification to select one element of the natural to stand for the whole. As a result the artistic convention has evolved which allows one element of a scene to dominate and carry the burden of mood and meaning.

Such a relationship between art and nature may have been one of the factors which encouraged the early film-makers to move out of the studios to natural locations. Certainly there is a direct link between the classical works of art and the way in which film-makers have treated nature in Japanese cinema, especially the use of a single element: the surface texture of soil in Uchida's *Earth*, the almost constant presence of rushes in *Sansho dayu* and the swaying marsh rushes in *Onibaba*, and, the supreme example, the sand in *Woman of the dunes*. In these the natural element is given such dominance that it effectively becomes as important a function of the film as any one of the players. The main reason that nature looks real in a Japanese film is because it *is* real. The treatment of nature plastically, which, in a European or American film, is always treated as a novelty by critics, is not seen as anything out of the ordinary by the Japanese since in their daily life they are aware of a deep inter-relationship between people and nature. This is not something foisted on the nation by any group of artists, but a cultural cornerstone of life. As such it is reflected in their films and gives them a particular

Bushido-Samurai saga (Imai, Toei 1963)
Figures moving unobtrusively into traditional compositions. The use of figures facing in opposite directions is frequent in Japanese films.

'look'. Because of this direct relationship between nature and humanity as expressed through art the Japanese have been termed the inventors of the pathetic fallacy.

The visual strength of the Japanese film also derives from a dependence on the eye rather than the ear which exists as an off-shoot of the way the Japanese language is written, and their distrust of the spoken word.

A heritage in the art of composition also enhances visual narration. The majority of Japanese films give the non-Japanese viewer an impression of careful image composition, yet look 'natural'. To a certain extent this feeling can be explained by the fact that many elements in the frame are composed parallel to the film plane. However this does not obtrude upon the consciousness of the viewer but subtly characterizes many Japanese films and creates an almost archetypal response.

When wide-screen formats were introduced to the cinema many cameramen in America and Europe felt ill at ease with its shape. Some thought that it was like looking at the world through a letter box. The Japanese, on the other hand, took to the wide screen as though they were born to it – which, on reflection, they were. Toho-Scope and all the other kinds of wide screen were simply a return to the format which can be found throughout the screen paintings of Japan and in the stage settings of Kabuki and Noh. With a sense of ease and familiarity Japanese cameramen used the wide screen to capture both the sweep of samurai sagas and placid interiors. In almost every case one senses that the wide format was organically related to the artistic heritage of the film-maker yet fitted perfectly to the modular format of the modern Japanese interior.

Colour came late to the Japanese screen. In making *Gate of hell* (1953) Kinugasa employed a modified form of the Eastmancolor process to produce clear pastel tones very like those found in old ink wash drawings. The effect was startlingly beautiful and enhanced the feeling of the twelfth-century setting. Miyagawa's colour photography for *Shin heike monogatari* marks the zenith of the use of colour in the Japanese film, and is correctly regarded as one of the finest colour films ever made.

Narrative structure in screen and scroll painting has been effectively transformed for use in the period film, actions being juxtaposed with little or no linking material, while the English-speaking stage, with a few notable exceptions such as John Whiting's play *The Devils*, has lost its links with the multiple staging of Renaissance painting and little of this style may be found in Occidental films. Yet, as can be expected of any major stylistic movement, there have been many variations and changes. In its more refined form the narrative style of *Shin heike monogatari* can be closely related to its origins in painting. Many of the more modern films with urban settings have maintained this narrative style only changing the samurai armour for flashy modern clothes, the swords for automatic weapons and the fiery steeds for gleaming motor cycles.

Once a style has been developed to such an extent that, even in its distorted forms, it permeates a medium, there often occurs a violent reaction against such formalism. Such was the impetus for many of the artistic movements in Europe: from the tremor of revolt in the Impressionists to the Dadaist paroxysm. Many young Japanese film-makers, influenced by the underground movement in America, have adopted a derivative form of narrative illogicality in reaction to what they feel is a sterile debasement of something once truly Japanese. While, in the past, few of these film-makers broke through into feature film production owing to the control exercised by the large studios, a growing number of co-operatives in Japan have created more opportunities for the experimental film-maker. In the last year or two the European and American festivals have been able to get hold of those films which are not being handled by the major distributors in Japan. Shuji Terayama, with *Throw away your books, let's go into the streets* (1971), managed to cross from theatre to films without a formal apprenticeship, almost unheard of in such a conservative industry, and shocked the audiences at the 1972 Cannes Festival. The same show contained his film *Emperor, tomato ketchup*. In each of these films he assaults his audience with a visual and verbal armoury, the like of which European audiences had not envisaged.

But the underground film-makers have in general failed to make any major break with traditional methods. The burden has been carried by some of the independent directors – especially Nagisa Oshima. As will be seen later, he has moved steadily away from the traditional narrative structure, adopting in the process methods which have a deceptive resemblance to those of Brecht and Godard, yet he uses an almost cartoon-like presentation of action peaks devoid of linking scenes, which turns out to be very similar to the traditional narrative form.

If the films, even the worst modern ones, have maintained an intrinsically 'Japanese' sense of composition about them, this traditional feeling for spacing and design, it is not for lack of contemporary examples to the contrary. The modern city-scapes in urban Japan must be some of the most aesthetically displeasing in the world. Japanese town-planning has produced some exceptionally ugly sights (but there is still a sense of shock to find a beautiful garden or a staggeringly simple temple in the middle of all this horror), yet there has been no noticeable use made of them in recent films with the exception of Terayama and a few others. Even Oshima for all his criticism of modern Japan is tempted to make the near-slum that lies behind Shinjuku look beautiful.

If we want to find a powerful revolt against traditional artistic concepts we must look at the work of the cartoonist, Yoji Kuri. Starting from a line drawing technique which has an honourable past in Japanese art he has

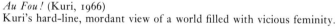

Au Fou! (Kuri, 1966)
Kuri's hard-line, mordant view of a world filled with vicious feminity.

refined his style into an acid hardness, which in its surreal world reaches the height of anti-art. One has a sense that his mordant view of humanity, as expressed in *Clap vocalism* and *Human zoo* (both 1961), *Love* (1963), *Aos* (1964) and *Au fou!* (1966), has led him to remove from his drawings anything that might be called beautiful by any common standards. Taking the sex war as his theme he presents a vicious portrait of mankind which contrasts sharply with the accepted Japanese self-image.

On the whole, though, cartoons are as traditional as the rest of the industry. Cartoons have been produced steadily throughout the history of Japanese cinema but only in the last ten years have they really come into their own. The development of electronic techniques has enabled a new feature industry to create a style which owes little to Disney in its surface texture and colour rendering, even though it has adopted many of the conventional Disney ideas on the plasticity of bodies, both human and solid. Based mainly on old fairy-tales or boy heroes in a futuristic world these cartoons make a delicate use of flat areas of colouring with little attempt at tonal shading, achieving a sense of depth and three-dimensionality by careful control of shapes and movement. The figures in these large-scale commercial cartoons, both human and animal, have a common feature that is rather unusual – large round or very slightly almond-shaped eyes. Made generally for a young audience such cartoons cover traditional folk legends such as Shinichi Yagi's *The Fox with nine tails* (1969) and under the direction of Daisuke Shirakawa, who has many feature cartoons to his credit, there has even been a cartoon version of that all-time favourite *The Loyal forty-seven Ronin*, called *Doggie march*, except that this time it is dogs against a wicked tiger and a fox, and the story has been transposed to a modern city setting.

Feature cartoons have not been confined solely to Japanese stories. In 1969 Kimio Yabuki directed a colourful if sentimental version of *Fables from Hans Christian Andersen* and in the same year Isao Takahata treated Nordic legend in a somewhat cavalier fashion by directing *Little Norse prince*. Although the figures have a sameness the animation of Yasuo Otsuka gives this film an exciting and dynamic sweep. Occasionally derivative influences show through, as in Taiji Yabushita's *Jack and the witch* (1968), which, whilst being a romping story, seems to have Disney backgrounds with UPA figures running around in front. Modern fantasy full of scientific wonders and strange monsters has found a champion in Cyborg 009, a boy robot invented by a Dr Gilmore who joins battle in film after film with the evil forces of the Black Ghosts. In films like *Cyborg 009* (1967) and *Cyborg 009 – underground duel* (1968) director Yugo Serikawa has made a modern equivalent to the samurai hero – protector of the good, destroyer of the evil.

Cartoons play a large part in the industry's production for television and are used extensively in commercial advertizing. Already a sizeable proportion of the work which is ostensibly produced by leading American and British animation studios is in fact jobbed out to Japanese animators and technicians.

Animation of this glossy and colourful type reached a maturity of sorts in 1971 with the production of a very explicit version of the *One thousand and one Arabian nights*. Unfortunately this startling piece of work has met with censorship problems overseas, but after the success of *Fritz the cat* (1972) it may be favoured with more liberal treatment.

From the science fiction and monsters of the cartoons it is a short step to the work of Ishiro Honda. In 1954 he started the cycle of Japanese monster films that is still selling around the world. Godzilla, however, was not the first monster to be seen on the screen for the demise of King Kong and Mighty Joe Young together with a variety of pre-historic beasts had already occurred. Honda, on the other hand, methodically invented a seemingly endless stream of fantastic monsters, each a cross between prehistory and a fertile imagination. Initially there was a definite political bias in his films, the monster in question usually being awoken from centuries of slumber by the careless use of atomic bombs, so that altruistic scientists (Japanese) battled with politicians of various hues as well as the monster to save the world. The anger and frustration with those who control the world's destiny and the potential for destruction that they held in their hands was scarcely disguised in the first few films but, whether from studio or personal pressures, Honda has allowed these issues to become submerged in special effects. His plots have become naive in the extreme and rather repetitive. After the original story had been overexposed a variation was introduced in the form of a friendly monster whose help is enlisted to assist the struggling scientists. Daiei got Shigeo Tanaka to make similar films, such as *Gamera v. Barugon* (1967), using the same formula as Honda. A new form of period film was discovered as giants and monsters were let loose in the period of the Civil War in such films as *Majin* (1967),directed by Kimiyoshi Yasuda. Toei then let loose a veritable horde of monsters in Tetsuya Yamauchi's *Grand duel of magic* (1968) and Nikkatsu made contemporary monster films such as *Gappa* (1968), directed by Haruyasu Noguchi.

The popularity of monster films has begun to decline but their success lasted more than a decade. In many ways they seem to provide audiences with the same sort of vicarious thrill as the extraordinary costume dramas that stream from the Shaw Brothers studios in Hong Kong. Like the Chinese films they are full of magic, blood and destruction, whilst the special effects which support the escapist element of the films almost submerge the plot. It appears that audiences throughout Asia have a need for such externalized violence and since the monster films fit neatly into a cultural heritage which

Frankenstein conquers the world (Honda, PCL 1966)

The War of the Gargantuas (Honda, PCL 1966)
Behind the gadgetry and special effects for the monster films lies a traditional set of moral values: good versus evil with the guaranteed triumph of good.

contains a heavy admixture of fantasy and violence, such films have become a perfectly acceptable form of sublimation. It is noticeable that some Oriental countries which have strict regulations in matters sexual will happily screen the most amazing murder and mayhem. The fantasy of the monster film became a safe way to express society's violence, until now when it is being pushed out by the more explicit violence of the gangster and 'pink' films.

15 Legacy of the Marquis

(*from*) *Farewell Before Dawn*

We have our work.
To work, we must talk,
But if we talk
The police come and batter in our faces.

Nakano Shigeharu (*b.* 1902)
Translated by:
Geoffrey Bownas
and Anthony Thwaite

The faster Japan climbs the ladder of economic success and the faster she changes the face of her urban life the greater the pressures grow on the individuals who live and work within that system. She has now created the modern city of Tokyo. Rising from the ruins caused by American fire-bomb raids Tokyo has spawned the biggest urban structure in the world. As large as Paris, New York and London put together this concrete fungus generates all the social ills that can be found in any major city, and complicates them by its size. Tokyo may not have the racial problems that beset the cities of America, though the Korean immigrants rest at the bottom of the caste system. Tokyo may not have to cope with vast numbers of homeless poor, as in Calcutta, or the shanty towns of Rio de Janeiro, but the slums of this gleaming city are a perpetual embarrassment to the city fathers. The size of the city and the chaotic numbering of houses has meant that papers and post may take days to deliver in some parts of town. The pollution problems are some of the worst in the world. There are areas of the city in which the pedestrian is given oxygen before and after walking through a half-mile dip in the road in which exhaust fumes gather. Policemen on point duty have a limit of twenty minutes before they return for oxygen treatment. Certain areas have been made traffic-free after the collapse of numerous children on the way to school as a result of the gases in the air. Traffic is reaching lunatic levels and at crossings pedestrians collect a yellow flag to wave at the cars as a warning as they cross the road. Housing is scarce and expensive, yet general standards in terms of material possessions are among the highest in the world.

There are many indications of the pressure on the ordinary man and the avenues of escape that are sought. In the fifties there was a rapid growth in Pachinco Parlours – arcades full of pin-ball machines. The playing of these machines, on which the player could never really win and what meagre winnings there were had to be claimed in consumer goods, reached epidemic proportions. Blank-eyed players flicked the steel balls for hours, even days, creating a mind-numbing clatter.

A Story of pure love (Imai, Toei 1957)
Romantic *Shomin-geki* in a contemporary setting.

The same sort of frustration was felt keenly by the young and intelligent, a frustration that exploded in the student riots of the sixties with their snaking, dancing ranks. To be young in Japan today, in a country which has made the Gross National Product into something close to a religion, is to exist in a puzzling world. To the end of his or her university days, including working for a post-graduate degree, the student must spend up to forty per cent of his time learning his own language. His study course is severe and the pressure to get into university is intense. Tokyo alone has nearly thirty universities and as a result the competition for jobs suitable for a graduate is depressingly fierce. Cramming schools hold classes of over five hundred pupils at a time for those trying to get into university – yet the pupil knows that when he has graduated he will probably occupy the fifth desk in the seventh row on the fourteenth floor of some down-town office. In time he will have a television set and a refrigerator but will still be a clerk. Japan's educational system gives her the world's highest literacy rate, 99.8%, and she publishes more books per head of population than any other nation. Naturally her highly educated intelligentsia seethe over the gap between what they know is possible and what they can do. In a country ruled by the Conservatives the students tend to be militantly left-wing, so much so that some groups consider the Maoists to be reactionary.

In the face of modern society it is not surprising to find the students in revolt, but the man in the street cannot really be said to share the same reasons for frustration. For him Japan poses the insoluble contradiction: a traditional set of values is denied by much of what is happening round him. He has long been told of his part in the larger group yet now he is submerged by the city so that he feels lost. The desire for group identity is satisfied for those who join one of the major industrial firms, but this is not possible for all.

Crime and the criminal society has burgeoned under these circumstances. The growing number of gangs have given rise to the *yakuza* or gangster film. However, these may be an expression of a social reality, but one suspects that the film companies quickly realized that they were onto a box-office winner. The silver screen provided the chance to romanticize the harsh and squalid reality of gang warfare and organized crime. The gangster has become the modern counterpart of the samurai, and the hero of the Kabuki play, the country boy who comes to the city and foils the wicked merchants, has become the lone avenger, young and handsome, who treads the border line between law and crime, and walks away into the sunset having executed a rough form of justice.

As a genre the *yakuza* tend to have a limited range of plots but are characterized by bloodshed and violence. Around the edge of the strictly 'gang' films grew a whole range of films about discontented youth, school drop-outs, drug addicts and tormented young love. Some even took the form of musicals, but the majority were much too savage for such a treatment. Narcotics, prostitution, extortion and revenge became the staple diet. Studios went to extreme lengths to capture the market in these films, some even using ex-gangsters as stars. Bernard Krisher, *Newsweek's* Tokyo bureau chief, even postulated that this was where the students had gone having failed to topple the establishment by riots and demonstrations. He quoted psychologists as saying:

'The *yakuza* are an outlet for aggressive feelings against the establishment. Young people in Japan have no faith in the future. They think everything is fixed; they have to pass exams, start as clerks, climb up the hierarchy. So they can imagine they are like the *yakuza* breaking out of the establishment.'

Kiku and Asamu (Imai, Toei 1959)
Imai's sincere consideration of a post-war problem: the mixed-race children fathered by American G.I's.

Noboru Ando, a film star who was himself a one-time gangster, gets nearer the reality of the situation when he says that the Japanese, indoctrinated from childhood with the belief that the group is more important than the individual, seldom do anything for themselves. The *yakuza* hero appeals to the Japanese because they admire (from a distance) a man who has the courage to act alone. So, paradoxically, people are living a conservative life yet sublimate desires to rebel into watching films whose heroes act rebelliously within a codified society as rigid as the feudal system and its code of *bushido*.

Yakuza films exemplify this contrast between the group identity and the individual but it is rare for them to present their characters in such a way that the viewer can ever really aspire to be that lone hero. He becomes so much a 'hero' that one may envy him yet stay a member of the gang. In such a context the film plays out in violent action the conflict facing each member of the audience in his daily life – the cultural contradictions of modern Japan.

A brief selection of *yakuza* films from recent years will serve to demonstrate some of the central concerns. Kinji Fukasaku's *Human wolves* (1965) showed genuine sociological concern in a film about three brothers who join rival gangs and thus place gang and family loyalty in direct confrontation. Kazuo Kawabe made *Classroom renegades* (1965) which whilst far from outstanding in artistic terms did exemplify a genuine social problem. In its treatment of the gangs of school drop-outs it falls into the trap of concentrating so much on its central characters, who are supposed to be bad, that inevitably the audience identifies with them and reaches the opposite judgement to what was expected. In the same year Masahiro Shinoda took the *yakuza* genre and using one of its standard plots – the young hero released from prison returns home to find that the gang structure has changed – turned a hack vehicle into genuine social protest. With customary visual brilliance Shinoda made *Pale flower* an objective, yet passionately concerned, attempt to examine and explain some of the motivations of the young who have been forced or led into the criminal underworld – for these are the extreme examples of many of Japan's younger generation who reject the values and conventions of their elders.

Fukasaka has continued to make action-packed gangster films, getting bigger budgets and venturing into wide-screen and colour in films such as *The Kamikaze guy* (1967). Series films emerged such as *The Filthy seven* (1968) and *The Return of the filthy seven* (1969) which despite the paucity of their plots about a gang used by the police to crush other gangs were sufficient to attract such stars as Tetsuro Tamba, hero of many a good samurai picture.

During the time that *yakuza* films were taking up much of studio production there was already a rapidly growing industry in 'pink' films or 'eroductions'. Initially these were strictly low-budget sixty minute films using out-of-work actors, models and anyone who was willing to take part. Made for the oriental equivalent of the dirty mackintosh brigade they worked to a strict formula of sixty minutes and one copulation every five minutes. That such films could be made and shown publicly is a result of Japanese law which, until July 1972, made censorship illegal. A committee existed with responsibility to restrain anything too offensive for public taste, but so ill-defined was their brief that there was little active censorship of any form. (In July 1972 the Japanese Government passed a bill to introduce restrictions on films, such as banning even simulations of the nude sexual act.) When 'eroductions' were first made there was no chance of television competing so they quickly gained financial success. However it may be that these films will follow the rest of the industry, for early in 1972 it was announced that some of the broadcast television networks were going to screen pornographic films after midnight and at the same time they could be bought in video-cassette form.

Once such films began to achieve commercial success the big companies turned steadily from the *yakuza* to 'pink' films. There had already been a highly charged sexual element in the gangster films and now this was increased as the gangster plot was faded out. Much of the ground was broken by small independent companies and they still stride ahead of the more conservative establishment firms.

There is a noticeable difference between the sex films of the West, whether soft-core for the cine-clubs or hard-core for the back rooms and American strip joints. In the Japanese versions there is something close to what the French film critic Marcel Martin describes when he says 'There is something that may shock innocent minds: eroticism cannot be separated from violence, as the divine Marquis has taught us.'

The sado-eroticism which fills these films, made by the young for the young, expresses the frustration felt keenly by this new sector of Japanese society. There are reasons deep in tradition for the form of this expression yet like so much in Japan they are fraught with paradox. In a society founded on the exploitation of man by man, and even more on the exploitation of women, there is no possible liberation for those who feel themselves to be oppressed except in the exploitation of those who have for so long been the exploiters. Violence is seen as a liberating force, as is the sexual act, yet the paradox remains that violence also oppresses and the sexual act can so easily oppress the female. One of Mizoguchi's films about prostitution, *Street of shame*, managed to balance the wisdom of the old with the idealism of the young. Contemporary directors of the 'pink' film reject such a balance, seeing even 'the wisdom of the old' as a vestige of an oppressive tradition. Yasuzo Masumura, formerly an assistant to Mizoguchi, considered the liberation of women in a violent world in films such as *The Electric Medusa*, *The Japanese cat* and *The Red angel*. In the latter film he concentrated on a nurse in a field hospital, whose erotic development springs from her confrontation with the horrors of violent and bloody death. Masumura, despite his high production rate of thirty films in twelve years, has remained a classicist in manner. The images have a memorable clarity of composition and the treatment of character is dispassionate in the most traditional way. However, if the form is classic the content most certainly is not. Putting his characters under the microscope he finds violence, sexual conflict and deviation beneath the surface of normality. To many Masumura represents the link between the conventional formalists of the Japanese cinema and the rebellious young, and there are those who look to him as a guide and mentor; he has certainly been a major influence on contemporary cinéastes.

'Pink' films, which in 1971 accounted for almost half of the nation's film production, vary from brutal stag films of the crudest sort to works of great craft and seriousness. It is regrettable that few, if any, of these films have been seen in Europe or America because of the restrictions of the censor. It is sadder still that when such films have managed to gain a screening they are marketed solely for their sexual content. Although many films can be loosely grouped under the title 'pink', there are also many better films which use sado-eroticism as a device to blast social mores and examine contemporary society and human relationships. *Mujo* (*This passing life*, 1971) directed by Akio Jissoji uses the context of incest, more explicit than anything made in Europe, in which to conduct a violent attack on Buddhism – or any form of organized religion – employing fantasy and dream to create a mixture which is, according to Max Tessier, more seductive than convincing. This use of a sexual context in which to conduct a serious argument is parallel to *I am curious — yellow*, modified by techniques derived from Brecht.

Other directors have chosen other paths in their exploration of human motivation. Often methods of striking severity produce films which are disturbing to watch but untrammelled in their intellectual content. Koji Wakamatsu, a leading exponent of the erotic film, took the true story of a mass murderer in New York who was driven by sexual obsession to rape, torture and kill eight nurses. Transposed as *Violated angels*, it becomes a catalogue of appalling horror, flowing with blood, yet it not only manages to remain objective so that all the events contribute to our understanding the demented murderer, but also, by avoiding all gratuitous images, it achieves an unbearable intensity.

The sadism which marks the films of Wakamatsu is remarkable in itself but should not be considered as either extreme or unusual. Virtually all the erotic films are coloured by such violence and the European sort of middle-class eroticism, which is 'tasteful' and often pleasant, is unknown in Japan. The sexual exploits of the suburban housewife and the prostitute with the heart of gold which flicker on the screens of Western cine-clubs have no place amongst 'pink' films. As in the *yakuza*, the 'heroes', often from the rural areas, arrive in the wicked city alone. They become ensnared in violent sex,

Violated angels (Wakamatsu, Shibata 1968)
An orgy of sex and blood by one of the leading makers of eroductions.

or are turned towards violence by their sexual experiences. Tetsui Takechi in *Black snow* (1965) showed a young man turned to obsessional murder after watching Japanese prostitutes and American servicemen making love, with the result that his impotence found release by literally making love with a loaded pistol. The Tokyo police seized the film and charged Takechi with 'public indecency'. He won both his case and the appeal with the counter-charge that the real grounds for accusation were the film's anti-American and anti-capitalist statements. *Black snow* may have opened the flood gates for subsequent erotic productions, but the seeds were already there in the cultural background and were germinating in the fertile soil of the *yakuza* films.

After the Takechi trial the court promised to keep a careful eye on future erotic films. It has taken seven years for any official reaction to make itself felt.

Although the phenomenon of the *yakuza* films has already begun to decline, it is not yet possible to predict the future for 'pink' films. It appears that there is a backlash growing in Japan against such productions, but something will be left behind. The liberation in matters sexual that was brought about by the eroductions has given Japanese films a chance for human and dramatic exploration and exploitation that cannot be fully destroyed.

Such a brief survey of a vast number of films can hardly do justice to the social importance of these genres. About 1500 films have been made in the last decade which fall within the boundaries of these classifications and are worthy of further study. One aspect that links these films is the attitude to death. For an individual to attain total freedom within Japan's ordered society the choice of death is perhaps the only true moment of liberation. Lovers dying together has for a long time been regarded as the supreme form of sexual ecstasy and indeed is a favourite theme of the Kabuki. Shinoda and Oshima among others have carried over this theme into films which examine the act of double suicide, but it has suffered an interesting sea-change in the transposition: death, whether in suicide or in the murder of the other person, is a declaration of personal freedom and is used as a cry of rebellion against established society. The traditional attitude to suicide still exists, the most notable example of recent years being Yukio Mishima's one venture into film direction in the somewhat narcissistic but horrifying version of his own short story *Patriotism* (1965), in which he also played the lead. His lovingly observed disembowelling on the screen was gruesomely prophetic of his own public suicide in 1971.

The young see Japan in a state of chaos to which one answer is death. In their films they attempt to give order to that chaos by expressing its outward form. This desire to create order and at the same time genuine art is most noticeable amongst the political left. The revolutionary aspect of their work is strengthened by the reaction of the conservatives and the liberals – those of the traditional right wing – who heap condemnation on the *yakuza* and 'pink' films. One thing remains certain. These new revolutionary film-makers cannot be ignored.

16 Extremes and experiments: the new wave

Stars

Over Japan there are stars.
Stars that stink like petrol
Stars that speak with foreign accents
Stars that rattle like old Fords
Stars the colour of Coca-Cola
Stars that hum like a fridge
Stars as coarse as tinned food
Stars cleaned with cotton wool and tweezers
And sterilized with formalin
Stars charged with radioactivity.
Among them, stars too swift for the eye
And stars circling on an eccentric orbit.
Deep down
They plunge to the base of the universe.

Over Japan there are stars.

On wintry nights –
Every night –
They stretch like a heavy chain.

Takenaka Iku (*b.* 1904)
Translated by:
Geoffrey Bownas
and Anthony Thwaite

From the confusion of the recent years certain independent film-makers have risen up like the waves of fresh cinematic talent that swept France, Poland and many other European countries. Today this freshness and vigour is driving forwards the cinema in South America. In the case of all these 'new waves' their directors have transformed the accepted classical cinema and given it new forms. In most cases the film-makers have the common characteristic of youth, but to go by critical reaction abroad, members of the new wave from Japan were bright young men. But critics had ignored the fact that the customary climb from the lowly ranks to the position of director usually results in a Japanese director making his debut at a much later date than in the West. It is strange to note that many of those who started out as independents are middle-aged in comparison to their overseas counterparts. Even Teshi-gahara, who was looked upon as a 'young' film-maker and had only spent a

The Island (Shindo, Kindai Eiga Kyokai 1961)
Water-carrying seems to impose a sense of order on apparently meaningless lives.

reasonably short time working in documentaries, was born in 1927. Masumura was born in 1924, Hani in 1928, Shinoda in 1931 and Oshima, one of the youngest of the group, in 1932. Kaneto Shindo was born in 1912.

Shindo is both a director and a writer, having written approximately fifty feature films in addition to his twenty-five or so directorial efforts. As a writer he has worked mainly for Yoshimura, and has scripted two versions of the famous Kawabata novel *A Thousand cranes*, directed by Yoshimura in 1953, and Masumura in 1969. As a film-maker he began directing with his own company, Kindai Eiga Kyokai, in 1950, and his early films were marked by their sense of social and political commitment, as in *Children of Hiroshima* (1952) and *The Lucky dragon no. 5* (1959), both of which expressed passionate opposition to the atomic bomb. *The Island* (1961) marked his recognition outside Japan, for in this film he presented a passionate but totally objective account of the lives of people living on an island without water. Much of their daily life is taken up with the seemingly senseless task of carrying water from the mainland across open sea, a few cans at a time – pitiful amounts with which to water the crops. Shindo achieved that identity with the soil that filled Uchida's *Earth*. He observes these struggling people in life and death and by his superbly controlled images and narrative pace enlarges their plight to represent that of the whole Japanese people. In 1964 a dramatic change occurred in Shindo's films with the introduction of sex. *Onibaba* continued his exploration of people in a microcosm, but the introduction of genuine eroticism blended with sadism radically altered the somewhat detached approach of his former work. Since then he has pursued this sexual line in *Lost sex* (1966), *Kuroneko* (1968) and the oddly titled *Operation*

Onibaba (Shindo, Kindai Eiga Kyokai 1964)
In a context of compelling sound and vision Shindo created a germane sado-eroticism.

negligée (1968). Unfortunately he tended towards sentimentality in these later films and did not manage to convey a genuine understanding of the sexual drives within a small enclosed society to the same extent as was shown by Imamura in *The Pornographer* (1966). He returned to form in 1970 with *Live today: die tomorrow* and *Heat wave island*. Both are thrillers, the first set in the gangland of Tokyo, the second in Tokyo, Kyoto and a small island. Either could have become banal action melodramas, but Shindo works within the conventional story format to produce in each case a searching socio-political examination of individual human beings.

Shohei Imamura is best known for *The Pornographer* which is the sympathetic study of an old man doing what he can for humanity through providing it with pornography. This strangely beautiful film ends unforgettably when the old man slowly drifts out to sea in his house-boat as he works on his ultimate invention – a rubber woman with imbedded hair. By putting his bizarre characters in calm everyday settings Imamura achieves a surreal effect which is more overt in his other films. *The Insect woman* (1965) is central to the entomological concern that figured in many films of that period, used by many directors as a device for close examination of Japan and the Japanese. Surrealism of a totally irrational kind can be seen in his film *Intentions of murder* (1964) with train doors opening onto raging seas, but the stylistic control of this surrealism achieved in *The Pornographer* was further refined in *A Man vanishes* (1967). Using a documentary technique and no actors he attempts to trace one of the many people who simply vanish each year in Japan. We are convinced that the person sought through interviews with his friends is a genuine human being – we even share in the accusation of murder made against a former girl-friend of the missing man. Yet this conviction can be smashed when in one scene the ceiling and walls of a room fly away to reveal a studio set. This concern with reality occurs also in *Kurage-jima: tales from a Southern island* (1968). Here, seduced by technique, the audience accepts the simple life on a somewhat primitive island to the south of Japan as an implicit criticism of modern society – a criticism which is shockingly hammered home when we jump forward from what seemed the present to the actual present, to see the island virtually destroyed by modern tourism.

Amongst the independent film-makers there has been a marked shift away from the style which has come to be recognized as most classically Japanese. There are perhaps no rules that can delineate this style, but there are elements which have become so common as to be regarded as trademarks of the Japanese cinema. These may be slight differences in pace from the films of other countries, a tendency towards a discursive and more leisurely exposition of character and plot, or even smaller details such as leaving the camera on a scene after the action has finished in an attempt to convey something of the pace of reality. Even in the fast-moving films of Kurosawa and Kobayashi the pauses exist, though shorter than is customary, giving the viewer a sign-post for the application of realist criteria.

The narrative style which marks out the newer films is one of great compression and speed. Much of this is due to the influence of Yasuzo Masumura, who although not an independent, has been looked to as the teacher of the

The Red angel (Masumura, Daiei 1966)
The story of a nurse's love for a surgeon in a field hospital takes on a new impetus in Masmura's rapid narrative.

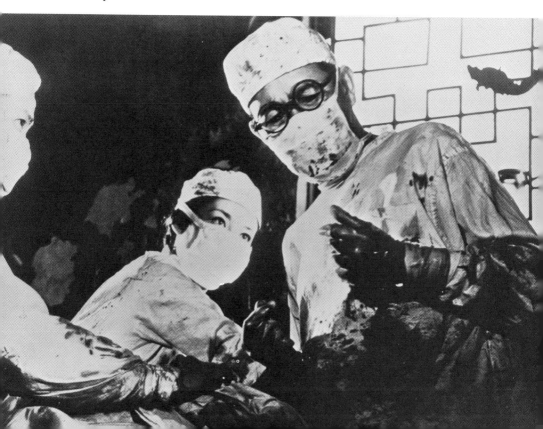

younger men. Born in 1924 he spent two years in Rome at the Centro Sperimentale from 1952 to 1954. On his return to Japan he worked as an assistant to Daisuke Ito, Kenji Mizoguchi and Kon Ichikawa. Add to this the influence of Yoshimura and the mixture is powerful enough to change the shape of films. From the great masters he has absorbed a sense of composition and flowing camera, and from his Italian experience he has developed a style of cutting from one peak of action to the build-up of the next peak of action. There are few pauses in his films and the sense of pace was a severe shock to Japanese audiences.

The narrative speed and excitement with which Masumura tells his tales is admirably suited to *The Red angel* and works perfectly for the virile excitement of *Hoodlum soldier* (1965) with its riotous story of two soldiers who both hate the army. The sharpness of his style added to the effectiveness of *Love for an idiot* (1967), the strange love story of an ultra-modern girl who manages to establish a happy sado-masochistic marriage. The same can be said of *The Build-up* (1958) in which his style matched the subject of corruption in the world of advertizing. However, as Donald Richie has pointed out, being subject to the will of a major company he has had to accept many less suitable scripts to which he has applied the same style producing much less satisfactory results. His influence is seen in the work of younger film-makers through the cutting rhythms of their films and in the way in which others are prepared to follow his lead in attacking many of the accepted and traditional values. As a stylist and an iconoclast he is a master to many.

Of the newer film-makers Masahiro Shinoda is the most outstanding stylist. He began his directorial career with Shochiku in 1960 but left in 1966 to form Hyogen-Sha. His first major film was *Pale flower* (1964), a melodramatic gangster film whose surface disguised an ellegorical dissertation on the downfall of man through the betrayal of his love. As Shinoda's reputation increased he was able to move away from the comedies on which he had cut his artistic teeth. He turned to domestic love stories such as

Hoodlum Soldier (Masumura, Daiei 1965)
Masumura's hard images and cutting speeds are ideally suited for his story of brutal army life (below), but they are too heavy-handed for the characterisation demanded in his tale of Lesbian love (right)

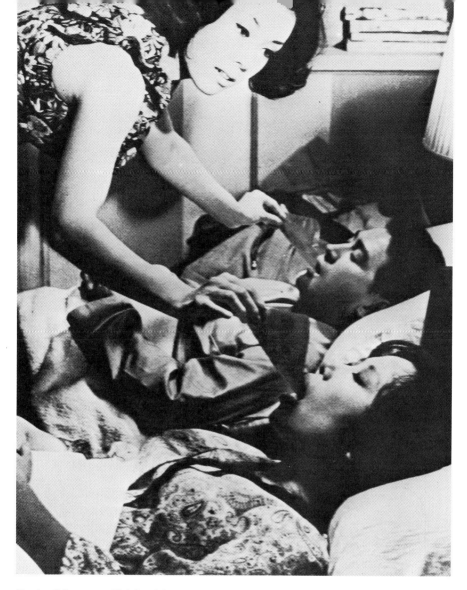

Passion (Masumura, Daiei 1965)

Kawabata's *With beauty and sorrow* (1965) and *Clouds at sunset* (1967). Both these films are concerned with the destructive nature of love and introduce the notion of destiny which was to appear in his later films. Both films gain enormously from the style of photography and beautifully judged cutting rhythms. Formal structuring of the domestic interiors creates patterns which are beautiful yet empty, devoid of any warmth that might sustain the love relationships. Images of death in the shapes of the vertical grave posts are stacked up by the camera lens – an overt sign of the death of human emotions.

All the elements with which Shinoda had been working came together in *Double suicide*: love and its destructive nature, and the inevitable workings of destiny as it controls the lives of two young lovers. Taken from a story by Chikamatsu of an ill-fated romance, the plot is treated by Shinoda in almost its original form. Since it was a Bunraku puppet play Shinoda uses the black clothed puppeteers on the screen to emphasize the way in which the pro-tagonists are being manipulated by forces beyond their control. Realism is rejected for the heightened style of the theatre, yet precisely because of this he

133

manages to achieve a greater credibility for the action that is played out before our eyes. Previous attempts to treat the puppet plays have aimed for realism and failed. Shinoda accepts the restrictions of the puppets and uses them to advantage. The story unfolds in disjointed scenes, the characters pushed

Double suicide (Shinoda, Shochiku 1969)
Stylized backgrounds and compositions fill this beautiful evocation of the *bunraku* puppet theatre.

hither and thither by the plot. Natural settings, unnaturally composed, are intercut with sets covered in huge blow-ups of wood-cut prints. Walls spin and fold away. The ever-present black-coated figures, their faces dimly seen behind the gauze masks, silently move furniture about and, like puppeteers, provide props at the right time. They appear to bind a hand, control the action in a fight, hold figures apart or thrust them together and in the end they impassively assist with the double suicide, the lovers' final revolt against society.

The artificiality of this style is essential to convince the audience of the reality of what is being said. In much the same way *The Scandalous adventures of Buraikan* (1970) takes the artificial style of its Kabuki original and makes it even more so. Though set at the end of the Tokogawa period amidst the confusion of a crumbling society, Shinoda's film creates a city so carefully artificial that it becomes a city of the mind. By imposing this style but hardly changing the original play he manages to build a viable parable about modern strife-torn Tokyo. In *Assassination* (1964), *Sarutobi* (1965) and *Silence* (1970) he has taken well-known historical episodes and substantially altered the meaning that they normally carry. The basis for most of these incidents is the conflict between duty and the dictates of the heart, and whilst this remains the motivation for the plot Shinoda shifts the attention to the pattern of life that is being worked out for, or by, the main characters. In this way he makes the characters relevant to modern society by using what was originally an ethically right wing situation as a means of studying an individual's problems, which is the approach of the ethical left.

If consistent style is Shinoda's hallmark, then lack of consistent style is the mark of one of Japan's most problematical directors. Nagisa Oshima achieved minor recognition for his films with Shochiku and then dropped out of sight for a while, so that in 1964 Donald Richie could write of 'the now forgotten Nagisa Oshima' when discussing directors working for the major companies. Fortunately, Oshima refused to become 'forgotten'. Originally he made films which seemed so disparate in style that little notice was taken of what his films were about. It was not until his later films, *Death by hanging* (1968), *Diary of a Shinjuku thief* (1968) and *Boy* (1969), received foreign distribution that critics began to see behind the apparent lack of continuity of style a solid continuity of themes and concerns.

Working within the *yakuza* genre Oshima seems to have recognized it as the ideal weapon for his particular attack on the values of modern Japanese society. In his early films, the realistic presentation of sex and violence provided the means to express dejection and depression with the present state of Japan. *A Town of love and hate* (1959) is filled with the social corruption which Oshima saw in Tokyo, with a community turning against an individual as a result of an unreasoning response to preordained social rules. *Naked youth/Cruel stories of youth* (1960) and *The Sun's burial* (1960) are both films set in the world of the Tokyo gangs, and as such appear to use all the accepted elements of realism. However, the surface texture is deceptive for whilst these films had little of the stylistic pyrotechnics that marked some of the later films they did have elements which signalled these changes to come and subtly altered the visual syntax of the realist gangster film. Peaks of action were often shown in long shot, leaving the viewer straining for information. Certain of the settings were so unusual as to be picaresque. A seduction scene in *Naked youth* is played out on the floating logs in the middle of a river, unsteady and shifting ground which parallels an unsatisfactory sexual relationship. A slightly surreal emphasis begins to enter these early films. All the factors mentioned served to shift the emphasis of communication from

The Catch (Oshima, Shochiku 1961)
Criticism of Japanese social values was already implicit in Oshima's early films.

the surface texture of the plot in terms of the visuals towards the verbal and ideological content of the films. Shock images of death mark these early films and there is a beautifully telling shot at the end of *The Catch* (1961) as a youth breaks away from the crowd watching the funeral pyre of an American negro and the youth's brother to light his own small bonfire of protest. From the very beginning, Oshima seems to have used, both consciously and unconsciously, the recurrent image of the sun, either in the form of the sun itself or in the form of the Japanese flag.

The sun floats over the log-strewn river of *Naked youth* (later echoed in *Death by hanging* in the strange scene of the Korean and his sister floating down the river on a raft, surmounted by an enormous setting sun). Much of the inner protest of this film was against the signing of the Peace Treaty with the United States, opposition to which was further marked by *The Sun's burial* and *Night and fog in Japan* (1960) – a series whose inner message records the declining hopes of left-wing protesters. Oshima has stated that he sees no direct links between the image of the sun and the Japanese flag, yet he uses both as symbols in his attack on the feudal and militaristic attitudes which he sees as current in Japanese life.

After making *The Catch*, Oshima dropped from the international scene for a few years, and though he has said that he was allowed almost total freedom by Shochiku he eventually departed to set up his own company, Sozo-Sha, in 1962. During these years he continued to make gangster films, but little is known of them outside Japan except his blending of the Chikamatsu story and a modern suicide in the film *Summer in Japan : double suicide* (1967) which has been shown in France, and his short film *Yunbogi's diary* (1965) which received a screening at the 1972 Edinburgh International Film Festival.

136

Oshima reappeared on the international scene with *Death by hanging* (1968). During the missing years changes had taken place in Oshima's style, but the central target remained the solid, traditional Japanese modes of thought and by implication the conservative government which encouraged and supported such an ideology. *Death by hanging* commences its severe monochromatic examination with an objective account of the mechanisms of execution in a Japanese prison. A condemned man is hanged after the due rituals have been observed. When it is found that he still is not dead the film moves steadily into fantasy, but a fantasy so shocking in concept that the importance of Oshima's subject is forced upon the viewer. The prison officials, including a Catholic priest, attempt to convince the condemned man that he is guilty of rape and murder, by re-enacting his crime and by re-constructing his home background, and therefore deserves to die. So, what might simply have been a sick joke becomes a savage attack. The story is based on the true case of a Korean condemned to death in the fifties. The plight of Koreans in Japan is not overtly stated in the film but it is essential to realize that they are treated as social pariahs by the majority of society for the force of the film's argument to be apparent. In the bare setting of the execution room, dominated by the Japanese flag, the re-enactment of the Korean's home life is a travesty exposing all the prejudices of the establishment figures. The condemned man is intelligent but has somehow been driven to rape an eighteen-year-old girl. As he watches the cavorting of authority and communes with his sister (either real or imagined), he comes to the inevitable conclusion that if the state finds him guilty then, since the state is plainly insane, he must be innocent. At the end he is hanged once more.

This stark and disturbing film not only indicts capital punishment, but, more importantly, an establishment run by the mindless puppets of its own

Death by hanging (Oshima, Shibata 1968)
The representatives of established authority look down dispassionately at the beginning of this Brechtian film.

creation, puppets who can be so carried away by their rôle-playing that they almost commit the act of murder themselves. By implication Oshima is saying that the state can no longer distinguish between reality and the rôle it has set itself to play, based on some outdated mythical ideas.

The narrative of this film shifts from reality to fantasy with no change in the visual style. Captions appear announcing the intention of the next chapter in a way which reminds one of Brecht. The influence of Godard can be seen in the structure of *Diary of a Shinjuku thief* as messages flash on the wide screen and the narrative leaps from one style to another. The story of Birdy Hilltop and his sexual inadequacy is a mixture of glossy 'realist' fiction, documentary both real and imaginary, and theatrical performance. A street balladeer provides a *benshi*-like commentary to this tale of disturbed youth, and the form of the film mirrors the confusion of this social group. Our acceptance of reality is constantly challenged by deliberate devices such as the use of poor technique during an interview – one can hear the camera and see the microphones in the frame. One expects some concrete statement but the inadequacy of the interviewee's answers only frustrates this. By the end of the film there is no longer any real distinction between truth and falsehood; the most severe test of this is the intercutting of a melodramatic scene, in which Birdy at last achieves the act of coitus, and scenes of student rioting and police brutality. Once more Oshima's targets are the social conditions which oppress minority groups and the hypocrisy of the older generations. The startling form of this film gave it much notoriety and a certain amount of excitement awaited the release of his next film.

When *Boy* was released in 1969 many viewers were surprised to find that

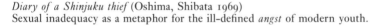

Diary of a Shinjuku thief (Oshima, Shibata 1969)
Sexual inadequacy as a metaphor for the ill-defined *angst* of modern youth.

Boy (Oshima, Shibata 1969)
The child as an emotional shuttlecock in a parasitic family; an indictment of traditional family values and their hypocrisy.

Oshima had once again changed his style. At first it looked like a radical reversal to a classical presentation, but the story slips easily into the fantasy world of the boy hero. As in *Death by hanging* the story is based on newspaper reports, this time of a family who for two years toured Japan using their eldest boy in a dangerous form of blackmail. The boy was trained to get knocked down by cars, after which the parents demanded money from the drivers in lieu of taking them to court. The film is built on a complex structure of references. Many of these occur in minor details like the change in the boy's school uniform which gives his age away to the ticket salesman at the station. The formal structure of the film throws a great deal of weight onto the recognition of these cultural signals and many of them might be lost on an Occidental audience. At the beginning of the film the boy is playing hide-and-seek with himself in a graveyard and his loneliness is emphasized when he loses the game. He sings a song linking a later scene in which his parents sing old wartime songs with a geisha. A contrast exists between the mother singing war-songs about dying for one's country and the supposed war-hero father getting drunk on *sake*: they live as parasites on the very society which they praise.

Throughout the film, whenever we see the family separated across a road or split by an argument, somewhere between them is the fluttering red spot on the national flag. This is a direct attack on the Japanese idea of the solidarity of the family – here shown in its corrupted form. Feeding off the modern world with its motor cars the family take every opportunity to revert to the traditional dress and style of living as soon as they have gained any money.

Despite the abuse heaped on the boy by his warring parents, at times he so tries to be like his father that he even wishes to emulate his father's injury. When a doctor says that a damaged arm may have to be removed, he replies 'Go ahead'. Yet the boy's desire to compete is tragic: he is being conditioned by his parents' behaviour to play a false rôle. In another scene the father strips to the waist to reveal his war-wound (which we now know to be fraudulent), takes up the posture of the period actor and then speaks in the exaggerated tones he has learned from the films. As do most of the characters, he borrows style to support a pose, the weakness of which is shown when the intrusion of a serving maid, whom we do not even see on the screen, stops him in mid-sentence.

Desperately the boy attempts to share a real emotion by scratching his hand to produce blood like the blood running from his mother's lip, after her husband has struck her. From this action follows a series of events which result in the death of a small girl and, although there is no causal link, the boy sees himself as the cause of her death. This leads to the central scene in the film in which the boy explains to his little brother that a snowman he has built – a sort of altar to the dead girl – is a man from Andromeda who has come to rid the world of all its bad people. Slowly the boy's sense of identification increases as he says that the snowman is all alone and that there will never be anyone to rid the world of its bad men. In his sorrow and desperation he destroys the snowman. Here Oshima uses the only trick in the film as he winds the camera gently into slow motion to create a genuinely moving sequence.

At the end of the film the boy cries, not for himself but for the dead girl and the whole hopeless situation. Oshima uses brief cuttings from newspapers to show that both parents were from disturbed backgrounds. But he does not thereby excuse them; rather he is accusing society of not helping them and of creating a situation in which they turned to crime as their only escape. They may be bad but society is worse.

In the film *The Man who left his will on film* (1970), sometimes called *He died after the war*, Oshima found yet another mode of exploring life in modern Japan. Using an amateur cast with a central character who could have been one of the students from *Shinjuku thief*, Oshima allows us to see the personal view of disillusioned youth. His hero sets out to make a film about his life, a search for some sort of personal truth within the apparently meaningless patterns of modern Japanese life. Like Yukio Mishima, the hero seems to be driven towards a known, planned and ritualized death – the act of making his film is the writing of a last will and testament. In the end we realize that the film we have been watching was to all intents and purposes the same film as the hero was making. In its critical view of certain sectors of Japanese life this film stands solidly in line with the thematic statements of Oshima's previous films.

Ritualized death, seen as a symbolic act for the death of Japan, figures in *Ceremony* (1971). The 'suicide' problem has been the theme of many recent Japanese films, standing as it does as a link to the feudal past and the code of honour. In a country which has become increasingly 'modern' and westernized the act of *seppuku* has focused the world's attention on the strained relationship between modern Japanese society and its past. Ritual suicide, serves as a dramatic device in *Ceremony*. The film works like a stone skimmed

opposite: *The Man who left his will on film* (Oshima, Shibata 1970)
A tapestry of images of a man making a film. At the end the viewer realizes that the film being made is the one he has been watching.

across the surface of a pond. In telling the complex story of a family the stone lands at those points in time when the whole family is gathered together for a marriage or a funeral, and at each point of contact sets up ripples which spread out across the face of society. As in *Death by hanging* Oshima has selected a group of 'second class' citizens through which to test many of the assumptions of society. In this case the family have returned from the former Japanese territory of Manchukuo or Manchuria, and because of this they are regarded by the rest of Japanese society as symbols of the imperialist past, and they still cling to outmoded forms of behaviour.

By selecting disparate moments in time at which to view the family meetings Oshima amplifies the steady influence of the western world upon the family traditions. Chairs and tables are introduced into formal seating arrangements and the wing-collared, frock-coated suits are replaced by soft collars and later by leather jackets. Each of the many ceremonies seen in the film exemplifies the struggle between the generations. Each ceremony is set up by the older members in accordance with tradition and each is seen as empty by the younger ones. In the end they too conform to ceremonial or ritualized patterns, either in the act of suicide, or in private and personal ritual. Masuo, the narrator of the film, having witnessed a ritualized 'marriage' in what Philip Strick has called 'a total fusion of love and death', retreats into his own ritual of an imaginary game of baseball ending by pressing his ear against the ground to listen to the cries of his brother who was buried as a child in the imperialist past of Manchuria.

In this extremely complex, but far from obscure film, Oshima appears to be making the statement that in the turbulent and perplexing world of today in which it is difficult to establish any sure foothold on reality there is a natural retreat into ritual. The older generations offer ritual to the young and the young take from these what they will. Oshima sees a society which has lost its sense of direction and looks backwards to the signposts that are to be found in tradition. What he also sees is that many of these rituals are empty, they have no real link with the past and therefore cannot provide any basis for the future.

His mode of expression is no longer the formal narrative of the earlier films. Here the cool and beautiful rendering of surface serves as a context for a delicately controlled surrealism. He draws no borderline between the normal and what expresses deeper psychological dramas. At a wedding the bride fails to appear, but rather than break with convention the older members of the family applaud her 'presence'. The groom reacts to her absence by usurping a corpse's place in a coffin and attempting a futile consummation. Oshima takes what is ceremonial within the Japanese structure and enlarges it by his own vision. He has stated 'Ceremonies are a time when the special characteristics of the Japanese spirit are revealed.'

Ceremony is a ravishingly beautiful film, shot in cool colour and filled with strangely compelling formal arrangements of characters, which, even if we do not recognize the cultural roots from which they have grown, show clearly the reliance on tradition and the hierarchical structure of the Japanese family. Philip Strick, in a review of the film in *Sight and Sound*, wrote:

'In one of the most beautiful scenes in the film – and there are many that are exquisite – the Sakurada family stands motionless around the body of an aunt whose love has been shared by three generations. The sword through her heart pins her upright to a tree. The splendour of this silent group, beside which the camera gently circles, is shockingly betrayed when one of the onlookers wrenches the sword free and two bright jets of blood leap from the corpse as it sinks to the ground. Ozu could have supplied the devoted members of the family. Mizoguchi could have supplied the elegant camera movement. Only Oshima could have added the blood.'

From the earliest days of his film-making Oshima has demonstrated his concern for the way in which he sees modern Japan developing. He attacks what he sees as social evil and injustice, yet these attacks spring from an intense awareness of what it is to be Japanese. In his recent films he has proved himself to be one of the world's most versatile directors, shifting his style in order to make the best possible exposition of what he has to say, but maintaining a thematic continuity. In that he is concerned with the very nature of being Japanese and he lives in a rapidly changing world, he shares the same place as Ozu, Mizoguchi, Kurosawa, Ichikawa and Kobayashi in the forefront of Japanese cinema. As a formalist, who can draw his styles from a wide range of sources and influences, he stands alone. Because of his stylistic inconsistency he has not yet become the leader of a 'school', and his individuality makes him atypical as a 'Japanese' film-maker. Yet his concerns make him the most important spokesman of a highly articulate group of film-makers.

Oshima's work has given strength and credibility to the independent movement in the cinema, and, although it may not yet present a threat to the 'big four' companies and the television giants, this group has attempted to shoulder the burden of artistic and intellectual leadership.

As in all arts, greatness is rare, and precious few directors in the cinemas of the world can be counted as great. The very nature of the film industry places commercial motivations high on the list, often diminishing or proscribing individual creative talent. Because of the size and structure of her industry – and her recent history – it would be remarkable if Japan had produced any really major cinematic talent. Yet it is too rarely recognized in the rest of the world that Japan's prodigious film industry has produced works of remarkable depth.

One can only guess at the future. If the big companies can survive the present recessions they will no doubt continue to produce 'tendency' films to accepted formulae. With increasing international recognition there is every chance that they will continue to develop major talents. If Japan imitates the pattern of the rest of the world then independent production may flourish. Film festivals will unearth more directors like Terayama. Japanese cinema has perhaps the most highly developed history in the world, which should ensure some sort of foundation for the future. It has produced some of the world's finest directors and its best films are artistic creations that rank with the finest that the rest of the world can muster. For too long the world has neglected the Japanese screen, for too long audiences have been denied the chance to see her work; now with the rapidly flowing tides of world change we cannot afford to ignore the words and images of her directors. Japan's cinema is a truly national cinema and as such stands as the outward expression of a nation's self-image.

Bibliography

General

Alex, William *Japanese architecture* Prentice-Hall International, London; George Braziller, New York 1963

Bownas, Geoffrey and Anthony Thwaite *The Penguin book of Japanese verse* Penguin Books, London 1964

Croot, Charles (ed.) *Japan miracle '70* Longman, London 1970

Fitzsimmons, Thomas *Japanese poetry now* Rapp and Whiting, London 1972

Hardwick, Michael *Discovery of Japan* Hamlyn, London 1970

Henderson, Harold G. *An Introduction to haiku* Doubleday, New York 1958

Little Library of Art nos. 21–4 *Japanese art* Methuen, London; Tudor, New York

Morris, Ivan *The World of the shining prince: court life in ancient Japan* Oxford University Press, London; Alfred A. Knopf, New York 1964; Penguin Books, London and Baltimore 1969

Piggot, Juliet *Japanese mythology* Hamlyn, London; Tudor, New York 1969

Price, Willard *The Japanese miracle and peril* Heinemann, London; Day, New York

Reischauer, Edwin O. *Japan: the story of a nation* Duckworth, London; Alfred A. Knopf, New York 1970

Storry, Richard *A History of modern Japan* Penguin Books, London; Baltimore 1960

Swann, Peter C. *Art of the world: Japan* Methuen, London; Crown, New York 1966

Varley, Paul H. with Ivan and Nobuko Morris *The Samurai* Weidenfeld & Nicolson, London; Delacorte Press, New York 1970

Wall, Rachel F. *Japan's century* The Historical Association, London 1964

Japanese Cinema

Anderson, J. L. & Donald Richie (foreword by Akira Kurosawa) *The Japanese film art and industry* Charles E. Tuttle, Rutland, Vermont 1959

Béraud, Bernard (ed.) *Japan independent film* Japan Convention Services Inc., Tokyo 1970

Estève, Michel (ed.) *Akira Kurosawa* Etudes cinématographiques nos. 30–31 Spring 1964, M. J. Minard, Paris 1964

Giuglaris, Marcel and Shinobu *Le Cinéma japonais* Editions du Cerf, Paris 1956

Govaers, Hiroko *Cinéma japonais* The Japanese embassy in France and the Cinematheque Française Autumn/Winter 1971

Hughes, Robert (ed.) *Film book 2: films of peace and war* Grove, New York 1962

Hughes, Robert & Donald Richie (ed.) *Rashomon: a film by Akira Kurosawa* Grove Press, New York 1969

Masumura, Yasuzo *Profilo storica del cinema Giapponese* Bianco e Nero, Rome 1955

Mesnil, Michel (ed.) *Kenji Mizoguchi* Cinéma d'aujourd'hui no. 31, Editions Seghers, Paris 1965

Richie, Donald *Japanese movies* Japan Travel Bureau, Tokyo 1961; *The Films of Akira Kurosawa* University of California Press, Berkeley 1965; *The Japanese movie: an illustrated history* Ward Lock & Co., London 1966; *Ikiru* (ed. and introduction) Lorrimer, London; *Seven Samurai: a film by Akira Kurosawa* (trans. and introduction) Lorrimer, London; Simon & Schuster, New York 1970

Schrader, Paul *Transcedental style in film: Ozu, Bresson, Dreyer* University of California Press, Berkeley 1972

Svensson, Arne *Japan* (Screen Guide series) Tantivy Press, London; A. S. Barnes, Cranbury, New Jersey 1970

A comprehensive bibliography of magazine articles on the Japanese cinema and on individual directors is contained in the library of the British Film Institute, Dean St, London.